GLOUCESTERSHIRE'S GREEN HERITAGE

Written and illustrated
by
Mary Hopkins

Barn Owl Books, Winchcombe, Gloucestershire   1989

GLOUCESTERSHIRE'S
GREEN HERITAGE

With thanks to Mike Hickey who taught me to
appreciate the beauty of plants

The publishers would like to thank Constable & Co. for permission to quote from "Country Contentments" by Margaret Westerling, Alan Sutton Publishing for quotes from "From A Cotswold Height" by John Henry Garrett, and Mr. P. Dobell for permission to use part of Eva Dobell's poem "Country Roads".

Published by Barn Owl Books, 33 Delavale Road, Winchcombe, Glos.

Mary Hopkins 1989.

British Library Cataloguing in Publication Data
Hopkins, Mary
Gloucestershire's Green Heritage
1. Great Britain. Plants
1. Title
581.941

ISBN 0 9510586 4 9

Phototypesetting, printing by Higham Press Ltd., Shirland, Derbyshire

Contents

Preface

The word 'green' has taken on a new and urgent meaning in recent years. It would be a pity, however, if the time-honoured implication of the word was lost, if only because, in including it in the title of her book, Mary Hopkins reminds us that Gloucestershire has a precious share in the heritage of 'England's green and pleasant land'.

Every hour we spend out-of-doors in Gloucestershire is enhanced by wild plants. Whether we drive, cycle, walk - or better still, stand and stare - the trees and shrubs, the flowers and ferns, the mosses and lichens - play a vital, if often overlooked, role in providing our pleasure.

Whether our location be in the Forest of Dean, along the Severn Vale, or up on the Cotswolds, these plants abound, as they have always done. True, many have been lost and others have become rarities, but the rich green mantle still covers Gloucestershire.

This book traces the part played by Gloucestershire's wild plants -in history, folklore, food, medicine, and in many other ways too -over the centuries. It is a pot-pourri of a book, rich in stories, snippets, smiles - and surprises. A strong sense of the past pervades almost every page.

Above all, it is a book that needed writing and it is sure to bring pleasure to all who love Gloucestershire and its green heritage.

Gordon Ottewell

Introduction

Gloucestershire is a scenically varied county. It ranges from the rolling downland of the Cotswolds, through the agricultural lands of the Severn Vale, to the Royal Forest of Dean. However, the landscape of today is not the same as that of yesteryear. It has been moulded by man to suit his needs.

In the early days of human habitation, the county would have been largely covered in the romantic-sounding wild wood — a dense tangle of trees with a herb-rich understorey, especially in clearings in the forest. By the neolithic period, man had domesticated animals which were allowed to graze freely in these woods. They fed indiscriminately on the herb-layer plants, taking not only those which seed quickly or resprout from freshly-nibbled shoots, but also the tree seedlings. Hence, there was nothing to replace the mature trees when they succumbed to old age. So, in a comparatively short time, the wild wood vanished, to be replaced by rolling grassland, marshy in the river valleys and windswept and stony on the hills.

This first man-made landscape has changed several times since those early days, perhaps the most drastic alterations occurring during the times of enclosures when the underlying patterns of the present field systems were laid out. Since then, there have been other changes, not the least of which happened in recent times when many hedges were grubbed up to make larger fields more suited to modern machinery. In forestry, changes have also been effected with the large-scale introduction of conifers.

Whatever these changes, Gloucestershire remains largely a green county, even its main towns are tree-lined and have extensive parks and gardens.

In times past, plants perhaps played an even more important part in man's life than they do today. They formed the basis of all medicaments, their fibres were used to make cloth, subsequently coloured with dyes derived from them, they provided food and could be brewed into potent drinks. It was the villagers themselves who collected the plants and transformed them into the varied end products, and so man was much more familiar with the green life around him than we are nowadays. The early gardeners also learned to use native and exotic plants to lay out formal and "natural" gardens, while farmers cultivated a wide variety of crops to satisfy both human and animal needs.

In former times, in the absence of any form of potted entertainment, folk whiled away long winter evening around blazing log fires talking and telling stories. The subjects covered ranged widely — gossip, legends of knights and damsels in distress, ghost stories and tales woven around everyday familiar objects. What formed a better basis than those familiar, yet beautiful flowers which grew on their doorsteps — legends telling where they came from, why they had such strange names, and how they had evolved into such wonderful shapes?

In this book, fact, fantasy and folklore of Gloucestershire plants have been drawn together in an attempt to throw some light on the forgotten (or perhaps unknown) green heritage of the county. It makes no claim to be a botany book, a county guide, or an identification book, but hopefully there will be something in it which will amuse or enlighten every reader, and above all awaken an interest in "Gloucestershire's Green Heritage."

PLANTS AND THE PAST

What's in a Name?

A study of the place names of any area reveals a great deal of the history of the neighbourhood — not usually the important events already well documented in historical records — but the social events. Many places were called after the families who lived there, others took their names from natural features in the landscape such as wells or springs, and some from the plants which grew in the vicinity.

Particularly fascinating are field names. It is not always possible to find records of these, but they are often listed in old documents. One difficulty in this study is that fields change name quite frequently, possibly with change of ownership, but also a name is often corrupted. For example, a meadow known in the early nineteenth century as Bancroft is the same as one which in the fourteenth century was Bencroft or the croft where beans were grown. This is merely a change of vowel but the alterations are often not so obvious as this and the origins of many names cannot be ascertained.

Fortunately, some names are little corrupted and from them we can learn quite a lot about Gloucestershire's green heritage. The use to which fields were put immediately after enclosure often gave them their name and so we learn that wheat, oats, barley and rye were grown in the county from names such as Wheat Leaze, Oatlands and Oathill, Barhill (bere = barley), and Rye Slade. More unusual crops which are revealed from local field names are vines from the Vineyard (several fields of this name occur across the county one of them being near Fairford), Hemplands (also near Fairford), Beanhill (Daglingworth), Flaxlands (Driffield) and Woad Ground (Great Rissington).

Hay was an important crop from the fields and this is reflected in the number of field names which refer to hay — Hay Hill, Hay Bank and Hay Meade. Some names even tell us more about the meadow. In Stowell, in 1811, was a field called Latter Math Meadow, this being the last meadow to be mown.

2

Bateman's Firs Little Bateman's Furze — Long Ground — Rook's Pool Piece — Fifteen Acres — Far Larch Ground — The Larches — The Forest — Rook's Pool — North Rook's Pool — Fourteen Acres — The Larch Ground — Charlock Ground — Near Rook's Pool — South Rook's Pool — Far Wold — Nine Acres — Far Cooks — Cooks Ground — Hollow Ground — Bush Ground — Pool — The Ash Ground — Thorn Well Ground — Hill Ground — Middle Barn Ground — Crab Tree Ground — Lower Barn Ground — Ground — Kineton Hill Field — Forty Acres — The Top Hill — Middle Hill — Clay Ground — Free Board — Lower Hill — Kineton Ground — Top Fox Hill — Kineton Thorns — Blind Well — Level Ground

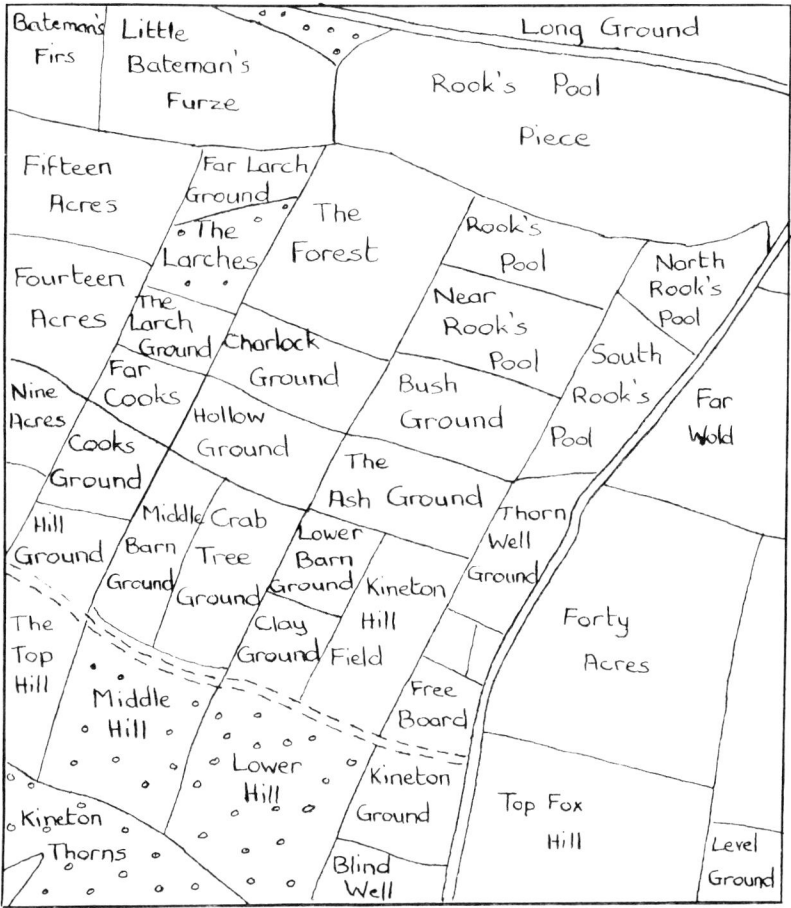

Field Names around Kineton

Withington obviously had some poor land for it had fields called Hungerstarve Meadow and Hungry Park. Rough ground often was covered with gorse or furze and this features in field names throughout the county. One of the earliest records is from Little Rissington where in 1217 there was a patch of land known as The Gorst. Other names include The Furze Hills, The Furzen, Furze Downs and Furze Brake. Nowadays, gorse is regarded as a menace when it invades a field, but in earlier times it was cut and used to fire bread ovens.

Many fields were called after the trees which grew in them. Consequently in the Vale there are many names incorporating the word elm — Elm Hole and Elm Hayes being examples. On the Cotswolds, the ash is more common and so we find Town Ash Mead, Ash Croft and Ash Grove to name but a few. Similarly oaks were important trees and give Oakley, Oaklands, Oakleaze and Gospel Oak, the latter possibly being a tree where a passage from the Bible was read during the beating of the bounds.

One tree which went under several names was the willow and from it we find Withy Bed, Withy Acre, Willow Bed, Witherhongers, The Willows, le Wythis, Sallowtree Furlong, and Osier Spinney. Other trees were obviously less common but when occurring made a good distinguishing feature for naming the field. The name Maplethorn was apparently derived from mapuldor or the maple tree while Eldern Slad was called after an elder. Pleasant to the ear is the field in Colesborne called Yew Yaw, but what horrors come to mind when picturing the Tetbury field which was called Nettlebeds?

As John Moore said in his book "The Countryman's England":-

> "This simple country fashion of naming places according
> to their associations and attributes still holds good in
> all the parts of England which are not yet suburbanized;
> and the old names of fields and woodlands, given to them
> long ago, are still used and remembered. You will not
> always find these places on the Ordnance map; you must
> search through musty plans in the offices of country
> solicitors and estate agents, you must listen to the
> talk of old men in the pubs or walk "round the cattle"
> with a farmer on his own land; . . ."

In a few hundred years time, surely, our modern practice of naming houses will provide the social historian with equally interesting information concerning our lives.

4

Vines and Wines

It is almost impossible to think of Italy without also thinking of wine. So it was that the Romans who settled in Gloucestershire brought with them vines which they found grew well in the slightly milder climate of those times almost two thousand years ago.

The vines continued to thrive in the county long after the departure of the Romans. Under the Normans, the Vale of Gloucester was considered one of the most favourable districts for wine and earned praise from William of Malmesbury:-

> "There is not any county in England so thicke set with Vine-yards."

He also added that the resulting wines

> "carried no unpleasant tartness, as being little inferioure
> in sweet verdure to the French wines."

The vineyards eventually came under the care of the monasteries, for example those of Winchcombe and Hayles, whose well-stocked cellars were famed for their excellent vintages, much as the chateaux of France are now known. It was claimed that the monks kept the best for themselves, selling the remainder to swell their coffers.

During the reign of Henry VIII, the cost of a barrel of English wine was ten shillings, compared to thirty-five for a comparable barrel of French vintage.

However, during a cyclic period of colder winters, the vines, which here had always been towards their northern limit of cultivation, succumbed to the long spells of snow and ice. Other starting materials for wine had to be found, and so the era of wines brewed in cottage kitchens from the native fruits of the English countryside began.

Michael Drayton wrote in 1613:-

> "But of her vines deprived, now Gloster learns to plant
> The pear tree everywhere; whose fruit she strains to juice."

Evidence of Gloucestershire's former pride is revealed in several local names, for example Vineyards Farm above Charlton Kings.

A Bunch of Flowers

We are so used to seeing huge floral displays in even the humblest of village churches and in most homes, that we forget the original "bunches" of flowers were simple affairs picked from the fields, woods or commons. They were often associated with children who carried them at various village events although grander arrangements began to be seen in churches in Elizabethan times. Candle-decked shrines had been removed by enthusiastic reformers, and in their place floral decorations began to appear.

It was the custom until fairly recent times, for children at a wedding in the Forest of Dean, to bar the way to the church with a rope lavishly decorated with bunches of wild flowers. The obstacle was not removed until the bridegroom paid over money to the culprits.

In another Forest custom, flowers were used to deck all the graves in a churchyard on Palm Sunday, as opposed to Easter Sunday in most parts of the country. The flowers were originally not placed in vases or containers as they would be today, but were spiked into holes in the turfed mound.

In Bisley, seven springs flow out of the hillside below the church. The water is directed into an ornamental trough and every Ascension-tide, this is the scene of the only Gloucestershire well dressing ceremony. This was introduced in 1863 by Thomas Keble and is much simpler than the better known Derbyshire ceremonies. After a service in the church, the children walk in procession to the springs carrying floral letters which are hung over the water outlets to make up the word "ASCENSION".

Until recent times, a mysterious bunch of flowers periodically appeared at the cross-roads known as Betty's Grave just outside the village of Poulton. No one knows who is buried there. One story relates that Betty was a witch who suffered death by burning, a second claims that she was executed for poisoning her employer, and a third that she was hanged for sheep stealing. In each of these cases, her body could not have been buried in the churchyard and would probably have been interred at the cross-roads outside the village.

Another idea was that Betty was a local, hard-working farm labourer who took on a wager to cut a field of hay in a day. Her prodigious strength carried her through the task, but the effort proved too much for on the way home she dropped dead, her body being buried where she fell near the cross-roads. Which ever of these stories is true, someone cared sufficiently to say "Well done", "Thank you" or "Sorry" in flowers.

Rush Strewing

Although, in the early days of the church, penitents may have wished to mortify themselves, it was no joke to kneel on hard stone or even trampled earth floors during long services. Consequently, it became the custom to cover the floor with dried rushes or hay in mimicry of the homes of the period where these natural coverings were used as early forms of carpet.

Once a year, these were ceremonially renewed often from a field bequeathed to the church by a grateful parishioner. In Medieval times this was probably a custom celebrated in most churches but now, in the times of efficient heating and embroidered hassocks, its occurrence is limited to a handful of parishes scattered across the length of the country. However, this practice, known as juncare, was still carried out in a few Gloucestershire churches into the later years of last century.

A mixture of hay and rushes were strewn on the floor of South Cerney Church, the harvest of lands bound by old regulations to supply these materials. When the ceremony was discontinued, the profits from the sale of the hay and rushes were paid to the church in lieu. In Tirley and Haw, the ceremony of juncare took place on Whit Sunday and Trinity Sunday, an acre of ground being given over to the maintenance of the custom.

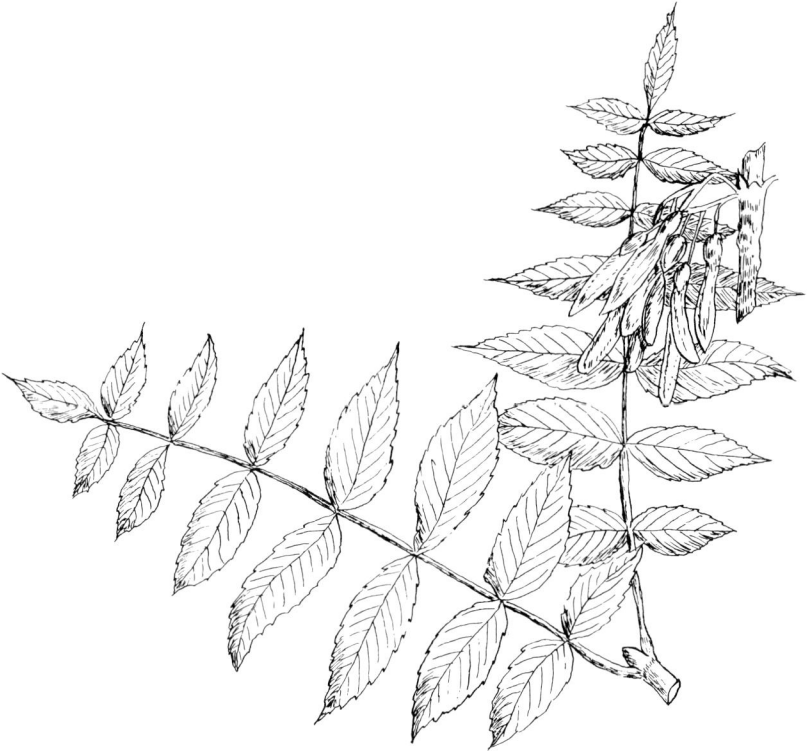

Pollarded Ash

Few trees, with the possible exception of willow, have been more subjected to pollarding than the ash. Pollarding is the lopping of the heads of trees in the hedgerow to stimulate the growth of many shoots from the cutting point. In time, these young, straight shoots can be harvested, which again encourages the growth of more young shoots. This cyclic cutting over many years results in a peculiarly shaped tree with a gnarled trunk surmounted by a "crew-cut" array of young shoots.

The wood of young ash is strong and elastic and has been claimed to be capable of bearing a greater strain than any other European timber of equal thickness. It has been widely used for carriage-poles, oars, hammer shafts, fence posts and ladders.

Although so much useful timber was produced by this practice, it was not universally acclaimed. A local diarist, J. L. Knapp wrote in 1829:-

"Prohibitions against mangling trees, in agreements, are usual; but, with some exceptions in regard to oak, little attention seems paid to the covenant, as is obvious on the most cursory view of the country in any direction . . . These prohibitions should not simply be engrossed on the parchment, but the agent ought strictly to notice any infringement; and young ash trees should be more especially guarded, because they are the most likely to suffer from their producing the greatest quantity of lop in the shortest time. . . . It is by no means an uncommon thing, to observe every ash tree in a hedge reduced to stumps by successive pollardings. Many a landlord would shudder at the thought of breaking up an old productive sward, and not regard the topping of an ash; whereas this latter act is infinitely more injurious ultimately than the former. The land may, and will probably, recover, but the tree is lost for ever, as to any profitable purposes for the owner . . . The ash, after this mutilation, in a few years becomes flattened at the summit, moisture lodges in it, and decay commences, the central parts gradually mouldering away, though for many years the sap wood will throw out vigorous shoots for the hatchet. The goat moth now too commences its mordications, and the end is not distant."

A Gloucestershire First

More than three hundred years ago, the first recorded greenhouse in England was built at Newnham by Sir Edward Mansell. It was heated with coal brought from the nearby Dean coalfield on the backs of strings of packhorses.

The Family from Frampton

The early Victorian era was an age which produced many famous botanical artists, both amateur and professional. Flower painting was considered a skill suitable for young ladies, and none demonstrated it better than the women of the Clifford family. They lived in the Severn-side village of Frampton, where their ancestors had been lords of the manor since Norman times.

The paintings seem to have created no sensation at the time they were completed, merely being consigned to the attics of Frampton Court where they lay forgotten until their chance discovery in 1982. Surviving were three leather-bound albums in which most of the paintings of wild flowers were mounted, and a considerable number of loose sheets with pictures of garden flowers.

Because many of the paintings were not signed, it is difficult to assess accurately how many people were involved in what appeared to be a family project to paint the flowers of the area. There were certainly three sisters, Catherine, Charlotte and Mary Anne, their two unmarried aunts — Rosamond and Catherine Elizabeth, and a married aunt — Charlotte Anne Purnell — the only one not to live in the village. Her home was Stancombe Park near Stinchcombe which lay about eight miles to the south of Frampton and extended the range of the flower painters. Probably, Charlotte Anne's daughter, Helen contributed to this joint family venture and also sister-in law, Marianne.

Almost three hundred flower paintings survived. The project must have followed a deliberate plan as there were very few subject repetitions. Together they painted over half of the wild flowers to be found in their locality. This was a considerable achievement as the landscape was so varied within a short distance of their home. Including the area around Stinchcombe, they painted plants from calcareous grassland, through woodlands, farmland, marshy regions to salt marsh, the latter being a rather specialized Gloucestershire habitat found on the banks of the tidal Severn.

The paintings are entirely water-colour and demonstrate both the use of superimposed washes, and also clever brushwork where the bristles are used as a pencil allowing very fine markings to be illustrated. Not surprisingly, the collection included paintings of few white flowers, a task which in those days would have been technically difficult because of the poor quality of the available white paints. More surprising is the omission of small plants of the hills around Stancombe Park — thyme, marjoram and salad burnet. In his recently published book — "The Frampton flora" — Richard Mabey suggests that this might be their personal reflection of the Victorian spirit, illustrating the ambivalence of that society which honoured domesticity and yet had a passion for expansiveness. In this vein, the artists painted the familiar, everyday flowers of the lanes around their home, and, in contrast, the rather exotic species such as orchids which grew on the Cotswold Hills.

Floral Design

"Tunley Lane was a great place for wild flowers. Periwinkle and deep crimson bloody cranesbill grew there, as well as a pink flowered wood sorrel, so at Gimson's suggestion I picked and brought with me a different wild flower each day and made a drawing of it. This was part of his training me in design and I soon found how differently one must look at a flower, or any other natural object, for this purpose. At first my drawings were as realistic as I could make them, with the accidental peculiarities of leaf and flower of the sprig I had brought with me, but he soon taught me to note only its special characteristics, making a simplified analysis of the basic peculiarities of the plant and then adapting this to a pattern suitable for modelled plaster, wood-carving or needlework as the case might be."

Norman Jewson
"By Chance I Did Rove"

The Weed

Tobacco was once an important crop in the vicinity of Cheltenham and Winchcombe. Both Raleigh and Drake who were largely responsible for its introduction to this country, had local connections. Richard Pate, the founder of Cheltenham's Grammar School, was a correspondent of Sir Humphrey Gilbert, brother-in-law of Sir Walter, and it is suggested that a parcel of the original seed brought from Virginia was sent to him.

No matter how started, it was found the plant grew well and was soon providing employment for many local people. However, in the seventeenth century, merchants began to complain of the great hardships suffered by the English plantation owners on the East Coast of America due to the great quantities of tobacco being produced at home. Consequently Parliament passed an Act forbidding the growing of the plant.

Within a month, the local growers sent a petition to Parliament. It said:-

"Humbly complaininge, sheweth unto your most excellent
Majesty and Parliament, your obedient and faithfull
servants, the growers and cominality of ye towns of
Cheltenham and Winchcombe: that your petitioners have for
many years past grown in ye comon fields ye weed called
Tobacco, and pray that your Highnesse and Parliament will
permitt them by your Council to practice the same, as
their crops will be perilled and lost, and it will be to
the ruin of very many labourers: our crops thereof
growing and growen also unto decay, with many other
inconveniences, in tender consideration thereof, may it
please your Majesty's Hon. Councell, according to ye
necessity of ye cause, and your said obedient subjects,
and all the countries round about shall accordingly pray
for your Highness and Parliament. Cheltenham, May, 1652."

The only result of the petition was permission to allow the harvesting of the crop already planted, but the growers were forbidden to plant more. However, this instruction was ignored and a troop of soldiers under Colonel Wakefield marched out from Gloucester to destroy the tobacco fields. About 500 locals faced them, threatening to kill men and beasts. Wisely the soldiers withdrew and it is believed no further action was taken against the growers.

In 1675, John Ogilby, on passing through Cheltenham reported that the people were "much given to plant tobacco, though they are supprest by authority."

Certainly, the cultivation of tobacco in the county did die out, but there are no records to show when the last crop was planted. The only reminder of the industry in the present day is a small, modern housing development on the Cheltenham side of Winchcombe which is known as Tobacco Close.

The Orchard Way

Hagloe Crabs, Blaisdon Reds, Blakeney Reds and Severn Banks — all these names are now more or less relegated to the horticultural historic record books for they were a few of the varieties of fruit grown on the west bank of the River Severn in past centuries. The orchards were mixed, most containing plums, pears and apples, consisting often of several different varieties of each of these. This ensured that all the crop did not ripen at the same time and that there would be no years when the whole crop was a total failure.

With the modern desire for standardisation, most of these varieties have disappeared, but it is only a continuation of a trend which extends back over the years. In 1789, a local writer was already bewailing the fact that so many of the local cider apples had vanished.

In the vicinity of Blakeney, the pears were used to make a red-tinted perry while in other parts of the region the brew was more conventionally coloured!

Herbal Signatures

Centuries of medicinal use have revealed the curative properties of many plants. Imagine, however, the difficulties of the first practitioners faced with an incredible array of flowers, seeds and fungi, convinced that in many of them lay the secrets of wonderful cures. Where did they start? How did they decide which plant to use for which illness?

Early herbalists believed that the answer lay in the strange code which became known as the Doctrine of Signatures. According to this, plants provided clues or "signatures" indicative of their medicinal function.

For example, the roots of celandine are knobbly, reminiscent of human boils, warts and particularly haemorrhoids. Thus a decoction of this plant was used to treat these ailments, and hence the derivation of its old Gloucestershire name — "Pilewort". Similarly, the leaves of lungwort bore marks suggestive of tubercular scars and consequently they were boiled to produce a tisane to ease the cough of a consumptive.

Colour was also an indication of use, so that blue plants such as speedwell or cornflowers were recommended for the easing of tired or weak eyes. (It is not recorded whether alternative plants were suggested for people with green or brown eyes!)

An associated belief was that the whole of life was governed by the Four Humours. This allowed the subdivision of all illnesses and their cures into categories associated with yellow and black biles, phlegm and blood.

When any disease had been correctly classified according to this theory, subsequent use of the Doctrine of Signatures indicated a possible cure. Illnesses caused by the yellow bile could be treated by yellow-coloured plants such as the buttercup. Black bile provided more problems as there are not many truly black flowers, but the difficulty was overcome by plants with black (or brown) spotted leaves. A plant producing white viscous sap reminiscent of phlegm, was used for ailments of the third category, while any diseases associated with the blood might be treated with red plants such as strawberries, peonies or rose petals.

14

Even the habitat of a plant could suggest its medicinal use. A person living in a damp place was liable to suffer from rheumatism. What better cure than one extracted from a plant which thrives in wet areas? And so an extract of willow would be fed to a patient suffering the agonies of rheumatism. The latin name for the willow is salix, and from this is derived salicylic acid, or asprin.

Similarly, docks and nettles often growing in harmony suggest the use of dock leaves as an antidote for nettle stings — a remedy still widely used.

There must have been thousands of mistakes made — patients poisoned by the injudicious use of plants, or their illnesses made more unpleasant by the enforced consumption of unpalatable brews. However, there must also have been a few successes, and by building on these shaky foundations, genuine herbal cures have evolved over the centuries.

Gloucestershire Plant Festivities

1st January
Exchange of New Year Gift Apples around St. Briavels (see page 75).

Twelfth Night
In Pauntley and Newent, farm-labourers gathered in a field which had been planted with grain. They lit twelve fires of straw around the perimeter of the field, one much larger than the rest. While the fires blazed, the men drank the health of their master and success to the coming harvest in tankards of cider. On their return to the farm, they ate caraway cakes soaked in cider.

Palm Sunday
This was the traditional day for putting flowers on graves in the Forest (see page 6).

May Day
This was widely celebrated throughout the country (see page 88).

Rogation Day
At Chipping Campden, the parson came out from the church to bless the fields.

Ascension Day
Well dressing at Bisley (see page 6).

29th May — Oak Apple Day

After the Battle of Worcester, King Charles II hid in an oak tree. The 29th May was both his birthday and the day when he re-entered Whitehall in 1660. On this date, children gathered oak twigs and sold them for a few pennies, a higher price being obtained for those bearing oak apples. Anyone not wearing a leaf was accused of being anti-Royalist, and even into the 1930s, children in village schools continued the custom. Those who failed to conform were chased by their school fellows bearing bunches of stinging nettles. This punishment was, by tradition, only allowed until noon.

Midsummer's Eve

This was traditionally a night when witches flew and therefore bunches of herbs including garlic, vervain and St. John's wort were hung over doors and windows to keep them out of the house. Frequently, these same herbs were thrown onto a bonfire, in the hope of driving away all unwelcome visitors from the village throughout the coming year.

Last Sunday in June

A fair with games and dancing was held in the cherry orchards in Synwell, near Wotton-under-Edge. A similar event was held at Saintbury in the North Cotswolds on completion of the cherry harvest. This was known as the Cherry Wake.

Sunday nearest July 10th

This was celebrated as Cherry Sunday in Gretton.

August 1st — Lammasday

Festival of the First Fruits (see page 82).

Mid-September

Harvest Festival (see page 83).

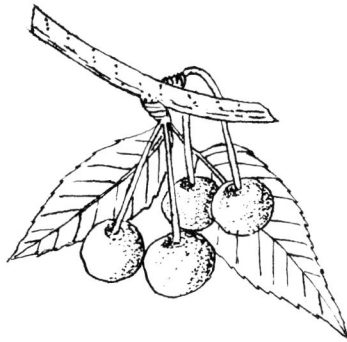

Sunday after 8th September

On this date the festival of Clipping the Yews takes place in Painswick. This actually has little to do with the famous yews (see page 60), but part of the service involves the children of the parish who hold hands to encircle the church. The word "clipping" is derived from the Anglo-Saxon meaning to embrace.

29th September

On this date, the City of Gloucester closed its shutters and went into the streets for the annual Barton Fair. It was the custom for private householders to hang out bushes of ivy, boughs of trees or bunches of flowers, as a sign that there was open house and a welcome would be given to anyone who cared to "drop in".

21st December

St. Thomas' Day was widely celebrated in the Cotswolds and was really a practical day for the poor who went round the village singing and begging for money or produce. Corn for making frumenty, and apples were usual gifts. A favourite song was:-

> "Please to remember St. Thomas' Day,
> St. Thomas' Day is the shortest day,
> Up the stocking and down the shoe,
> If you an't got apples, money'll do.
> Up the ladder and down the wall,
> A peck of apples'll serve us all."

24th December

At midnight, people watched for the blooming of the Glastonberry Thorns (see page 84).

25th December

One of the few days still celebrated by bringing greenery into the house following a tradition practised for centuries.

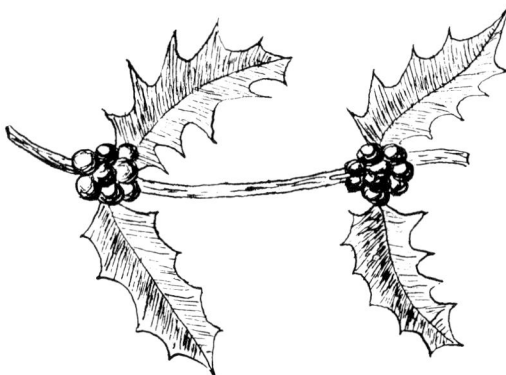

18

The Wars of the Roses

One of the bloodiest battles between the Houses of York and Lancaster, occurred in Tewkesbury, on 4th May 1471. The Lancastrian, Margaret of Anjou, had marched her troops from Weymouth to meet their allies from Wales. However, before this happened, they were intercepted by the army of Edward IV and the Battle of Tewkesbury took place in the fields surrounding the town.

It is difficult to pinpoint the exact site of this battle between the Red Rose and the White — in fact there were probably skirmishes over a wide area, but all records mention the Bloody Meadow, a field lying to the south of the modern town, not far from the present day Council Offices.

Margaret watched from the tower of the Abbey as hundreds of her men were slaughtered. Some sought sanctuary in the Abbey itself, but even these were later executed at High Cross in the town. The Queen escaped but was later captured near Malvern from where she was escorted to London where she arrived on May 21st, the same night that King Henry VI was killed in the Tower.

This left the crown in the hands of the Yorkists who kept it until 1485 when Richard III was killed at the Battle of Bosworth Field.

It seems ironic that flowers — usually the symbols of peace — should have been used as the emblems of the opposing sides during those troubled times.

The Tewkesbury Borough Council have created a circular trail around the battle sites, including the field still known as Bloody Meadow where they have planted white and red thorns together with willow and alder in memory of those who fell so long ago in this Gloucestershire battle.

When Flowers Spoke Volumes

In ancient Mediterranean civilisations, flowers are known to have been used as a means of communication. For example, a master handing a slave a rose, immediately freed him from any further servitude.

A basic flower language had evolved in this country by Elizabethan times. Shakespeare said of Ophelia, "... with fantastic garlands did she come, of crow-flowers, nettles, daisies and long purples ...". Translated, these flowers described her as a fair maid who was stung to the quick, her virgin bloom under the cold hand of death.

Later, a more sophisticated version of the language of love was introduced from the harems of Turkey by an eighteenth century poetess and traveller — Lady Wortley Montague. It reached the height of its popularity during the straight-laced period of Victorian times, when courtship had to follow a prescribed ritual and any open display of feeling was forbidden. Careful choice of flowers in a posy and their arrangement could express any desired sentiment. How messages were conveyed when the necessary flowers were out of season remains a mystery, except in February when a delicately painted bouquet on the front of a Valentine's card could say far more than any sentiment expressed inside.

In his book "A Wanderer's Gleanings", John Farmer describes his meeting with a girl called Trixie on Painswick Beacon. She wished to know about the language of flowers and so picked a small bunch of plants growing on the hillside and asked him what they meant. He took them one by one giving her the following answer:

> "Rye grass means a changeable disposition; rock roses tell of
> popular favour; daisies are emblems of innocence; meadow grasses
> denote submission; and buttercups ingratitude. The
> interpretation therefore reads: "A changeable disposition often
> meets with popular favour, while innocence and submission
> engender ingratitude"".

In response to these ideas, a modern youth would probably offer a saffron crocus — a token of mirth!

Plants and Places

Tree-lined Town

The Times once described Cheltenham's famous Promenade as "perhaps the most beautiful thoroughfare in the country." Nowadays, it is not only that famed avenue, but the whole town which revels in a year-round display of floral beauty — an event which has several times in recent years made it winner of the 'Britain in Bloom' competition.

About thirty years ago, a report stated that one in every ten acres of its area was occupied by public parks and floral gardens maintained by the Corporation, with many more acres of privately owned, well-kept gardens. There were also forty miles of tree-lined roads accounting for 40,000 individual trees. A one-time Medical Officer of Health for the town, John Henry Garrett, once wrote "In Cheltenham trees and houses go together as if by nature."

This reputation indeed goes back to the days of the late eighteenth and early nineteenth centuries when the town was gaining its reputation as a spa. Up till then, it had been a mere rural village straggling along the banks of the diminutive River Chelt. The first mineral-rich spring was found by a flock of pigeons who enjoyed the crystallized salts left in a field when the spring water evaporated. An observant onlooker realized the potential of the waters and from that day the town grew in importance.

As new springs were discovered, gardens were laid out around them and visitors flocked from near and far, not only to take the waters but also to stroll in the parks.

The next phase of the town's development was its growth as an educational centre with the establishment of famous schools, colleges and churches.

All these facets are incorporated in its coat-of-arms, Cheltenham being one of the few towns in the country which can, and quite rightly does, boast of its sylvan beauty.

Branch's Cheltenham

At the turn of the century, a Cheltenham resident, Henry Branch, who had spent some time in India, came back and gathered together many articles he had written both in exile and at home. They were published under the title "Cotswold and Vale" and provide an interesting insight into life in those times, especially in Cheltenham. The following extracts throw light on the leafy character of the town.

"It is in the Spring when Cheltenham, always fair to look upon, puts on her best. Then it is that her title of "Garden Town" is supremely justified. "I have visited many towns in England," said a friend of mine, as we drove down the Promenade to Pittville one May morning, "but none so beautiful as this."

"The air is laden with the incense of tender shoots; the sunshine, broken by sylvan fretwork, falls in golden patches upon the roadway, and gleams on lime and chestnut, birch and beech and elm; while, thanks to the lilacs, hawthorns and laburnums, growing freely in the gardens and enclosures, there is abundance of colour and contrast amid the green of the surrounding foilage."

"Let me return to the limes, the copper-coloured beeches, the firs, the ever-green oaks which line the leafy ways of Cheltenham and throng her pleasant spaces. The Montpellier Gardens are looking as always in the vernal months, charmingly arborescent, particularly near the Pump Room, while the few flower beds, which suffice in grounds of this character, are bright with flowers."

"Pittville Park must be regarded, after the Promenade, as the leading "attraction" of Cheltenham. Here Municipal ownership and control has effected in recent years, a vast improvement; and when Spring lays her magic hand upon the place, it becomes a beauty spot worthy of the nearest approach to the ideal Garden City which England, at all events, can show."

A Tree Lover's Estate

The year 1829 saw the start on open agricultural land of what is now one of Britain's most famous collections of trees — Westonbirt Arboretum. Its design was personally supervised by the owner of the estate, Mr. Robert Holford.

His lay-out was intended to show trees from all round the world, not only as individual specimens, but in groups so that their form and colour were perfectly displayed and contrasted. The site was ideally suited to such an undertaking as, not only did it have large areas of a limey soil, but also smaller patches of greensand, enabling a wide variety of tree species to be grown.

Initially, commoner trees such as scots pines, oaks, cherries, laurel and yew were planted to provide shelter for more delicate specimen trees. These, at first, came mainly from California and Japan. Holford particularly loved conifers and the gardens boast almost every species of conifer known at that time.

In 1892 Robert died, to be succeeded by his son George who fortunately had inherited not only the estate, but also his father's interest and talent. He had already worked with his father for about twenty years during which time they had planted Silk Wood, a region of oak with hazel under-storey.

When left to his own devices, George Holford worked with renewed enthusiasm and added large numbers of rhododendrons and oriental maples to provide the dazzling Autumn colours for which Westonbirt is famed.

By the start of the present century, new species were being brought back to Britain by intrepid collectors, and a collection of ornamental trees with decorative bark and flowers was begun.

Lord Morley was the next owner of the Arboretum and Silk Wood, the house having been purchased by Westonbirt School when it was founded in 1928. Planting was continued under the supervision of his curator, W. J. Mitchell.

Lord Morley's death in 1951 left the future of the estate in some doubt. Fortunately, in 1956, the Forestry Commission stepped in and now care for this wonderful collection of trees which is open for anyone to enjoy.

The Oak Monarch

Each county has its famous trees, not necessarily the biggest or oldest, but for some reason beloved by local folk. Gloucestershire boasts several, four of them being oaks, namely those of Boddington, Lassington, Painswick and Newland. All of these have now been felled but each in its time must have been a sight to behold.

The one at Boddington was quite hollow, its shell being converted into a circular room. Sadly this tree was destroyed by fire in 1790.

The best known was probably that at Newland, and the following description by a local tree expert, Mr. J. W. Stanton, gives a pleasing picture of the giant during its declining years in the 1890s.

> "The Oak Monarch at Newland, in the Forest of Dean, is the largest in girth and probably the oldest of its kind in Gloucestershire. It is in an orchard about half a mile west of the church, and is forty-three feet in girth and forty-two feet high, a mere shell, with some fine stag-headed branches standing well up from the living outside rim. It is a good specimen of conical growth, the original stem having probably been broken off short by storm and wind hundreds of years ago, and decay having in consequence slowly but surely consumed the heart which is now represented by a hollow of six feet diameter. The exuberant growth of bark in convoluted masses supports such life as yet remains, and gives this oaken bowl a unique and picturesque appearance. The tree must have been thriving at the time of the Norman Conquest."

The tree finally fell in a gale in 1956.

Cleeve Residents!

There were two trees growing near White Hall (on Cleeve) which went by the names of John Oak and Betty Ash.

Royal Forest

Now successfully managed by the Forestry Commission, the Forest of Dean has undergone many changes in fortune. These events have largely been caused by conflicts of interest, the Dean being a Royal Hunting Forest, a rural area where people kept herds of pigs and flocks of sheep, and an industrial region where coal and iron have been mined and iron smelted.

In the twelfth and thirteenth centuries, the Forest of Dean was a well-established royal possession with its own courts and officers. Not only did the King use the woods as a hunting ground, but also owned forges in the region. Records show that by 1300 between 40 and 70 forges were working, their demand for charcoal greatly impoverishing the woods.

In Medieval times, this loss of trees continued, natural regeneration being negligible because of the tradition of allowing animals to graze in the Forest. They nibbled off both sprouting seedlings and the young shoots from newly coppiced trees.

By Tudor times, the Crown was seriously alarmed about a possible shortage of timber for warships. An Act was passed in 1559 forbidding the felling of oak, beech or ash as timber for charcoal-making within fourteen miles of the sea or a navigable river. It is believed that this was largely aimed at the Forest of Dean which was one of the biggest culprits in this field.

However, other records suggest that during the sixteenth century, the timber potential of the Dean was considerable, so much so that it was rumoured that the Spanish admiral in charge of the Armada had given orders that the Forest of Dean should be destroyed even if the whole of England could not be conquered.

Eventually, in 1612, water-power arrived in the Forest to drive the bellows of the forges. This meant that even greater volumes of charcoal were required and it was this demand which initiated one of the most violent periods of Forest history and almost resulted in the destruction of Dean as a tree-growing area.

Commoners objected to enclosures of land where they traditionally had grazed their flocks and gathered wood. The riots began in Mailscot Wood near Bicknor where fences were taken down and five hundred people demonstrated in front of the homes of land agents.

Even worse rapes of the Forest were to follow, Sir John Winter being the prime offender. In 1640, he was granted "all coppices, wood, ground, and waste soil of the Forest with the Wood and Timber, and all the Mines of Iron and Coal, Tin and Lead, and Quarries of Millstones, Grindstones and Cinders in the Forest." During the period of this, his first lease, he reduced the Forest trees from 129,000 to 88,000. During the Civil War, Winter was deprived of his property and sent to the Tower for defending the Forest for the King.

However, he survived his time of confinement, and, after the Restoration of the Monarchy in 1662, his rights (and more) were returned to him, giving him an excuse to continue his devastation of the Forest. His tree-felling activities were so severe that Parliament unsuccessfully tried to interfere to save the remaining trees. In fact, four years later, he was given yet another lease which allowed him 8,000 acres for himself and the management of another 10,000 as a nursery for naval timber.

Employing 500 woodcutters he soon felled all but 200 of the trees on his own lands, and delivered to the navy only 1,000 tons of the agreed 11,000 tons. The remainder had been cut, but where it had gone is open to speculation.

Further devastation was caused at this time by two great storms which destroyed much of the remaining timber.

Eventually, in 1668, an Act of Parliament settled Forest affairs. It gave the Crown the right to enclose 11,000 acres on a rolling basis allowing the enclosure of young plantations. The Commmoners lost their grazing rights in these areas, and firewood collection rights throughout the Forest. In exchange, they were given pannage and grazing rights in the rest of the Forest. It is this Act which still largely governs the Forest management of today.

A further Act of 1808, initiated systematic planting and in the next ten years four million young oaks and 88,000 ash, elm, sweet chestnut and fir were planted.

In 1823, a visitor wrote:-

"I rode about the Forest, which 50 years hence will be a real Forest;
at present it consists of about 11,000 acres of young plantations
six or seven years old, but where the oaks are growing luxuriantly."

All the careful planning, however, did not work out as expected. The oaks, of which so much had been expected, were found to be poor specimens.

In 1896, a forestry expert wrote:-

"Any person with a pair of eyes, found on by far the greater part of
the area, a thin crop of oaks from 80-90 years old, of poor height growth,
with rounded or flat tops, and the branches coming down low, so that only
clear boles of small length are formed."

The writer, Sir William Schlich, compared these trees with the few remaining massive oaks left from earlier centuries, wondering what had brought about the change. His conclusions were that the old oaks had been planted in a mixture of beeches and oaks, and that by planting oak alone, the fertility of the soil had been reduced. It was from this time that more thoughtful management of the Forest began, a policy which was continued when the Forestry Commission took over in 1919.

About 3000 acres of the early nineteenth century planting remains, but most has been felled and replanted with a carefully controlled mix of broadleaved and coniferous trees. The oaks are managed on a 150 year rotation, conifers being felled generally after 50 or 60 years.

Despite the ups and downs of Forest fortunes, we are fortunate in Gloucestershire to have kept this large historic area of woodland, still governed by an administration which partially dates back to Medieval times, the only other surviving example in England being the New Forest.

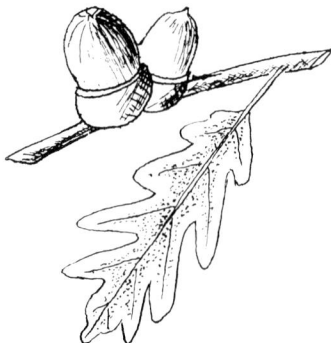

The Genius of the Thames

The south-eastern corner of the county drops down to the pleasant water meadows of the stripling Thames, an area still reasonably rich in wild flowers despite modern attempts to squeeze as much profit from the land as possible. How much richer it must have been in the early days of last century when Thomas Love Peacock penned the following lines:

Where Kemble's wood-embossed spire
Adorns the solitary glade,
And ancient trees, in green attire,
Diffuse a deep and pleasant shade.
The bounteous urn, light murmuring flings
The treasures of its infant springs,
And fast, beneath its native hill,
Impels the silver-sparkling rill
With flag flowers fringed and whispering reeds,
Along the many-coloured meads.

Sweet is thy course, and clear, and still,
By Ewan's old neglected mill:
Green shores thy narrow stream confine,
Where blooms the modest eglantine,
And hawthorn-boughs o'ershadowing spread
To canopy thy infant bed.
Now peaceful hamlets wandering through,
And fields in beauty ever new,
Where Lechlade sees thy current strong
First waft the unlabouring bark along.

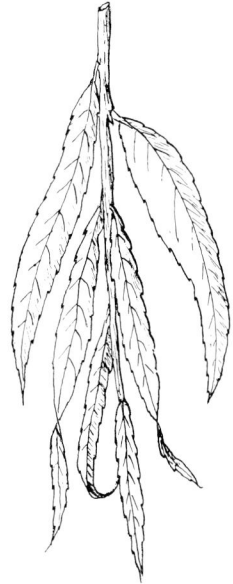

29

A Wooden Spire

Westbury-on-Severn is one of two Gloucestershire churches with a detached tower. This was originally built in the thirteenth century as a watch-tower to give early warning of Welsh invasions which still occurred from time to time.

In the seventeenth century, the tower — obviously no longer needed for defensive purposes — was converted by the addition of a fine spire. The framework was made of an intricate array of great oak beams taken from the nearby Forest. It was 160 feet high and when first built contained no metal. Even the tiles were of wood, supposedly made from the staves of casks which had held cider. This must say something of the preservative qualities of the local brew, for the shingles lasted almost three hundred years until 1937 when they were replaced by a new set of 60,000 oak tiles, this time held in place by copper nails.

Abbotswood

The inclusion of the word "Wood" in a place name may often seem strange when nowadays there are no, or few, trees to be seen in the vicinity. However, the name is probably centuries old and tells us something of the history of the area.

Such a place is Abbotswood, which lies just south of Cinderford. Legend relates that Henry II on a visit to Flaxley Abbey gave the monks the right to feed both their cattle and pigs in the Forest of Dean, to take sufficient timber for maintenance of the Abbey, and to fell two oaks per week as fuel for their forge.

Even monks can be guilty of the sin of greed, and over the years began taking far more timber than their privilege allowed. Henry III heard of this and took away their rights to Forest timber, in exchange giving them 870 acres of woodland near Cinderford, hence the name Abbotswood.

Most of the woods have now vanished, though whether this was again due to excessive tree felling by the monks, or because of later land management, is not recorded.

Ag Pag Dump

"Nympsfield is a pretty place
Set upon a clump
And all the people eat there is
Ag Pag Dump."

These strange words are inscribed on a plaque in Nympsfield Church. Traditionally, the dump or boiled pudding was eaten on St. Margaret's Day (20th July), but in fact it formed a good, economical and nourishing pudding which could be used to eke out a meagre meat ration at any time of year.

Most of the ingredients could be gleaned from a hedgerow or cottage garden, and the recipe could be altered according to the availability of the herbs.

The base of the pudding was barley boiled until it softened. To this was added a beaten egg and a little butter. Colour and goodness were provided by a mixture of chopped herbs including onions, nettle tops, watercress, the leaves of sorrel, blackcurrant and dandelions. A herby tang was obtained using a sprig each of mint, thyme and sage.

Lines inspired by the road between Coln St. Aldwyns and Fairford

See the soft green willow springing
Where the waters gently pass,
Every way her free arms flinging
O'er the moist and reedy grass.
Long ere winter blasts are fled,
See her tipped with vernal red,
And her kindly flower display'd
Ere her leaf can cast a shade.

Isaac Williams

31

A Water Garden

The reign of William and Mary marked a phase in gardening much influenced by Dutch styles. One of the few remaining examples of the popular water gardens during those times can be found at Westbury Court on the west bank of the River Severn.

It was laid out between 1696 and 1705 by Colonel Maynard Colchester, and includes a straight canal with a pavilion at one end, and a parallel canal having a T-shaped opposite end. The brook which originally flowed through the garden was diverted round and used to feed the canals.

The accounts for the planting of the gardens list the purchase of 2,000 yews, 1,500 hollies, Scots pines, filberts, laurestinus, tuberoses, phillyreas, both espalier and standard fruit trees including plums, cherries, pears, peaches, apricots, nectarines, and grapes. Flowers recorded were tulips, iris, crocus, jonquils, hyacinths, narcissi, honeysuckle, mezereon, bay, asparagus, anemones and ranunculus. Payment was also made to a weederwoman!

Besides plants, the garden has a stone figure standing on an island in one of the canals. Legend tells that this is Neptune who climbs from his pedestal to bathe when he hears a neighbouring clock strike. Another tradition claims that the statue is an image of a river god found in the Severn, possibly washed up from the Roman temple at Lydney.

A delightful feature is the provision of iron-work peepholes, so that the casual passerby might enjoy a momentary glimpse of this garden of a bygone age.

The formal straightness of the canals, geometric flower beds and neatly clipped yew hedges were all features of this type of garden, subsequently superseded by the casual informality of curved beds, and long avenues of trees framing distant vistas. In 1712, in Gloucestershire, twenty big houses were recorded as having a Dutch water-garden, but Westbury Court is the only one to survive undisturbed through the later fashions.

Water Lilies

"And what flowering plants can be more beautiful in form and hue than the Water-Lily, whether it be the pure white, or the richly golden, or the gorgeous red, with their leaves floating, heart-shaped or oval, on the placid surface, and the charming flowers just rising amid their circular grouping, and reflected petal for petal on the glassy face?"

A Gloucestershire Wild Garden
The Curator (1903)

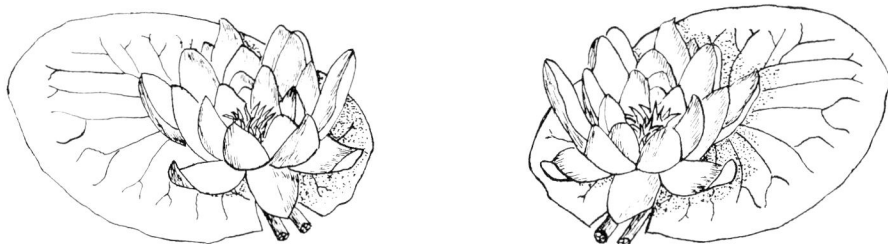

Profitable Plants

"There are several white Water-lilies, old and new, and the indigenous one, Nymphea alba, is not the least in value, nor to be slighted because it is an old friend. Its only fault is that it is too generous, and its tendency to increase must be curtailed, for if allowed to unduly crowd itself, it loses much of its charms. Yet this tendency to increase may be turned to account. I find that I can realize a guinea a year from one pond alone by judicious thinning out and sending the well-grown roots to the nurseryman, who retails them at double the price he gives me, and thus the increase affords me the means of adding one or more of the expensive species annually to my collection. This is prosaic, but useful."

A Gloucestershire Wild Garden
The Curator (1903)

33

Cirencester Park

Standing at the spot known as Ten Rides in Oakley Park which forms part of the vast Bathurst Estate, one can appreciate on what scale the grounds of Cirencester House were laid out during the eighteenth century. During the course of a long life, Lord Bathurst, who died just before his ninety-first birthday, changed the whole face of the area. He converted what had been open downland into Oakley park, by enclosing, planting, transplanting and even altering the land contours by cutting away and constructing hills.

He was a friend of many literary men of his day, but perhaps more than any, the poet Alexander Pope was a frequent visitor to Cirencester. He aided and abetted Lord Bathurst in his arboreal pursuits and encouraged him in the building of a series of follies in the grounds. Perhaps most spectacular of these is Alfred's Hall, a sham ruin. So realistic is this, that it is said when a guide was showing visitors round the park during Lord Bathurst's lifetime, on seeing their delight, she told them that the ruin was a mere nothing and invited them to return in a few years time when there would be another ruin, at least two hundred years older!

The parkland has now matured and the plantings of the eighteenth century are venerable trees. The long straight rides have been maintained, the biggest one — Broad Ride — being almost five miles long and fifty yards wide. It runs from Sapperton to Cirencester, the church tower of the latter being visible along its whole length.

By kind permission of the Bathurst Estate, the public are invited to walk through the woods to enjoy this great park covering 3000 acres, and marvel at the foresight of an eighteenth century politician who did not live to see the beauties of his fully matured estate.

Pope's Answer to a Conversation With Lord Bathurst

"Wood's are — not to be too prolix —
Collective bodies of straight sticks.
It is, my lord, a mere conundrum
To call things woods for what grows under 'em
For shrubs, when nothing else at top is,
Can only constitute a coppice."

The Golden Cotswolds

Tragically, J. Arthur Gibbs, a lover of the Cotswolds, died at the age of 31, in the last year of the nineteenth century. Fortunately, he left us one classic work — A Cotswold Village — first published in 1898.

The following extract is typical of some of his marvellous descriptions of the countryside and people around his home at Ablington, near Bibury.

"The prevailing colour of the Cotswold landscape may be said to be that of gold. The richest gold is that of the flaming marsh-marigolds in the water meadows during May; goldilocks and buttercups of all kinds are golden too, but of a slightly paler hue. Yellow charlock, beautiful to look upon, but hated by farmers, takes possession of the wheat "grounds" in May, and holds the fields against all comers throughout the summer. In some parts it clothes the whole landscape like a sheet of saffron. Primroses and cowslips are of course paler still. The ubiquitous dandelion is likewise golden; then we have birdsfoot trefoil, ragwort, agrimony, silver-weed, celandine, tormentil, yellow iris, St. John's wort, and a host of other flowers of the same hue. In autumn comes the golden corn; and later on in mid-winter we have pale jessamine and lichen thriving on the cottage walls. So throughout the year the Cotswolds are never without this colour of saffron or gold. Only the pockets of the natives lack it, I regret to say."

Places to Visit

No matter how enthralling a book about plants, there is nothing to beat actually getting into the field and seeing them growing either in their natural habitats or in a formal garden.

The following list includes just a few of the gardens open to the public at certain times during the year. Opening dates and times should be ascertained before a visit.

Barnsley House — in the village of Barnsley, 4 miles N.E. of Cirencester.
Batsford Park Arboretum — 1.5 miles N.W., Moreton-in-Marsh.
Berkeley Castle Gardens — Berkeley.
Cirencester Park — Western side of Cirencester (open free of charge to pedestrians throughout the year — no dogs).
Hidcote Manor — Hidcote Bartrim, 4 miles N.E. Chipping Campden.
Kiftsgate Court — N.W. of Hidcote Bartrim.
Lydney Park — 0.5 miles W. of Lydney.
Snowshill Manor — In Snowshill village, 3 miles S. of Broadway.
Sudeley Castle — Winchcombe, 6 miles N.E. Cheltenham.
Westbury Court — Eastern edge of Westbury-on-Severn.
Westonbirt Arboretum — Westonbirt, 3.5 miles S.W. Tetbury.

Many other Gloucestershire gardens are open at certain times of the year under the charitable National Gardens Scheme. A yellow book called "Gardens of England and Wales" is published every spring listing these gardens and their opening dates.

Plants in their natural habitat can be seen virtually anywhere in the county, from rubbish dumps, through flood meadows via Cotswold grasslands to the woodlands of the Forest of Dean. The following list includes a few special places with easy public access.

Bourton-on-the-Water Gravel Pits — 1 mile E. Bourton.
Chedworth Woods — 7 miles S.E. Cheltenham.
Cleeve Hill — 4 miles N.E. Cheltenham.
Coombe Hill Canal — 3 miles S. Tewkesbury.
Cotswold Water Park — South Cerney, 3 miles S.E. Cirencester.
Cranham Woods and Buckholt Woods — 6 miles S.W. Cheltenham.
Crickley Hill — 4 miles S.W. Cheltenham.
Forest of Dean — West of River Severn.
Golden Valley — between Chalford and Sapperton.
Leckhampton Hill — 2 miles S. Cheltenham.
Gloucester & Sharpness Canal — From Frampton-on-Severn to Sharpness.
Guiting Wood — 2.5 miles S.E. Winchcombe.
May Hill and Newent Woods — 3 miles S. Newent.
Queen's Wood — 3 miles W. Newent.
Stinchcombe Hill — 1 mile N.W. Dursley.
Tewkesbury Ham — Tewkesbury riverside.
Wye Valley — From Symonds Yat south to Chepstow.

The Severn Ham

Every winter, the River Severn is liable to flood, inundating acres of low-lying land on which it deposits fertile mud carried from upstream. The area subject to this annual flooding is now much diminished due to a system of embankments and improved land drainage which rapidly carry the waters back to the main river.

At one time, all these areas formed rich water meadows where, during the summer months cattle grazed knee-deep in wild flowers beneath a sky ringing with bird-song, all combining to form a landscape which seemed to epitomise the best of England.

The Severn Ham, an island of meadow land between the River Severn and the Mill Avon, is one of these few remaining regions. It is still managed in a traditional manner, being owned by the Tewkesbury Town Council. They sell the grass at auction each year. After the haymaking, which should be completed by the 12th July, the grass is left to grow for one calendar month after which the Aftermath, or Right of Pasturage, is sold also by auction. The grazing animals may be left on the Ham until the 13th February, after which they are removed to allow the grass and its associated flowers to grow.

It is this regulated management, unchanging from year to year, which allows the development of the rich, varied flora for which the Ham is famed. Naturally a diverse flora, in its turn, supports a rich insect life and consequently, a good bird population.

Village Name

Saul lies on the east bank of the River Severn, south of Gloucester. Obviously, at one time, willows thrived in the vicinity for the name is supposed to be derived from "Salley", a word still used in local dialect for the willow.

PLANTS LARGE AND SMALL

The Pasque Flower

To find this delightful spring flower is a special treat and worth the miles of walking probably necessary to seek it out. It is a plant of undisturbed, grazed, limestone pastures and once was much more prolific on the traditionally managed Cotswold sheep-walks than it is today.

However it is worth hunting out this relation of the better-known wood anemone or windflower. Under a cloudy sky, it remains almost closed, but when the sun of April or early May shines on it, the flower opens to reveal a wonderful violet-purple colour. Each stalk carries only a single bloom, relatively large for the height of the plant (often only two or three inches), but the most conspicuous feature of the plant is its silky hairs which clothe the outer surface of the flower, giving the unopened buds a satiny sheen.

A frill of finely dissected leaves surrounds the stalk about half-way up. They close around the bent head of the growing bud, but stand upright when the flower reaches maturity. The true leaves appear as the flower is fading and the central tuft of seeds develop a silky plume of feather-like hairs.

The name "Pasque" refers to the Easter season, and yet in this county the plant is rarely in full flower by then, although before the change to the present calendar, it must be remembered the seasons were eleven days different to what they are now. The flower gives a bright green, clear dye which in former times was used to colour eggs given as Easter gifts, a custom which in this country has largely been replaced by the giving of commercially-made chocolate eggs. Ancient records relate that four hundred eggs were purchased for decoration for the royal household of Edward 1.

According to an old Gloucestershire tradition, the Pasque Flower only bloomed where Saxon blood had been spilled in battle!

Pasque Flower — Protected Bloom

"Perhaps the flower in greatest danger is the pasque flower, that beautiful anemone which does not lurk in woods and which waits until the last spring snow has really gone, and the cold Easter winds are at any rate softened by the May sun, before raising its purple head above the turf of the exposed sheep pastures which alone it loves. It has not too many resting places in the land, and it is gregarious in its habits, so that it is easily assailed in bulk when discovered. In this locality I know of several attacks upon it with basket and trowel, out of sheer love unfortunately, so how is the assault to be averted? ...I beg anyone who goes to hunt for the pasque flower with trowel and basket, or even with a simple pocket-knife, to think of them as living gems passionately attached to their native home, and before digging a single root to ponder first very earnestly."

Algernon Gissing (1924)
The Footpath Way in Gloucestershire

The Daffodil Crescent

"From Marcle Way
From Dymock, Kempley, Newent,
Bromsberrow, Redmarley, all the
Meadowland daffodils seem
Running in golden tides to Ryton Firs."

So wrote Lascelles Abercrombie, a poet who adopted Gloucestershire as his home in the years before the First World War.

Unfortunately, nowadays, the delightful wild daffodil is not present in such numbers as it was when it inspired these verses. Probably the main reason for its decline was the great change in farming practices especially during the years of the Second World War when vast areas of the region which was known as the Daffodil Crescent were ploughed up as every available square foot of land was used for food production.

Such treatment soon resulted in diminishing numbers of flowers which could only find respite in the hedgerows and woodlands. Here too they found themselves under threat as people flocked in from miles away, not only to admire the sight of a sea of swaying daffodils, but also, for the payment of a few pence, to pick armfuls of the blooms.

Indeed, the railway companies ran special trains — The Daffodil Express — from both London and the populous areas of the industrial Midlands to this largely unknown corner of Gloucestershire. The damage was done when during the picking process, visitors pulled the stem right from the heart of the bulb rather than snapping it off above ground level.

Fortunately, before the daffodils — or lent lilies as they are known locally — were completely destroyed, modern conservation ideas were implemented and these small versions of our common garden varieties now enjoy protection so that everyone can enjoy the wonderful sight of daffodils blooming in woods, orchards, hedgerows and a few fields. They have even spread onto the banks of the M50 motorway — a case of man and nature existing side by side.

A Useful Herb

To most modern palates, tansy has a bitter, unpleasant taste, yet in former times was much prized as a flavouring. On Easter Sunday, when the leaves were young, it was used to make tansy pudding served with, for those who could afford it, the traditional roast lamb. It is claimed by some that this was a reminder of the Passover feast with its bitter herbs, but others think that it was used because of its medicinal properties which counteracted the richness of the lamb partaken after the lean season of Lent.

Tansy cakes were also made around this time of year and were given as prizes in sports such as stool-ball and hand-ball. These games were a sign to the village folk that the long cold days of winter were over and the more pleasant, though busier days of summer had begun.

Women found other uses for tansy. It reputedly had "the power to restore feminine beauty, however faded, to its former freshness". It was laid in buttermilk for nine days, the resulting liquor being subsequently used to annoint the face.

On a more practical note, meat was rubbed with tansy leaves to repel flies. The main disadvantage of this was that the meat afterwards was highly flavoured, especially in the later months of summer when the full aromatic potential of the leaves had developed. Consequently, other strong spices had to be used in cooking to counteract the taste of the tansy.

Less damaging to the flavour of food was the hanging of bunches of tansy mixed with elder leaves from the kitchen rafters to repel flies. Similarly, tansy was often one of the strewing herbs scattered on the floors of houses or churches, was used in nosegays carried to keep the plague at bay, and was rubbed into the coats of dogs to rid them of fleas.

The Fair English Rose

Perhaps the best-loved of all British flowers is the rose, both the garden varieties and the humble dog rose which enlivens our hedgerows in the early summer. It was frequently used to decorate Gloucestershire churches on St. Barnabas' Day (11th June) and was said to fade by the feast day of St. Mary Magdalene (22nd July). A dog rose, precocious enough to bloom in Autumn , was said to portend an epidemic during the approaching winter.

The colour of this wild rose, in its bud stage, ranges from deep pink to a delicate blush, but fades almost to white as it opens fully.

On close inspection, many people are surprised to find that the prickles of the dog rose point downwards. These actually help the rose to climb up and gain support from surrounding shrubs. Legend, however, has a more picturesque explanation.

44

When Lucifer was evicted from Paradise, he tried to regain entry by climbing back up a rose tree. At this point in the story there are two versions. In the first, God stunted the growth of the rose so that it never again grew into a large tree whose upper branches could reach to Heaven. In his frustration, the Devil turned the prickles round so that they pointed earthwards rather than towards the goal he could never reach.

In the second version, the Devil used the prickles, which at that time curved upwards, as a ladder. When God saw him nearing Heaven, he turned them round so that their curved profile could not be used to provide a foothold.

According to old custom, roses were planted on the graves of young people who died after betrothal but before marriage. A walk around many Gloucestershire churchyards will reveal several, long-neglected roses still blooming on graves whose epitaphs have been obliterated by the combined action of weathering and lichen cover.

In Dowdeswell churchyard, after the First World War, as an unusual tribute, a standard rose was planted for every man of the parish who had been lost in action, the roses lining the path leading to the church door.

Medicinally, the dog rose had many uses. Its root was supposed to cure rabies — one suggested reason for the prefix "dog".

Hips were much prized when garden fruit was scarce, and could be used to give acidity to any bland dish. They were also made into a cordial, much used in World War II as a vitamin-rich drink serving as a substitute for the unobtainable orange juice.

There were few parts of the dog rose which found no use. The leaves were made into a tea, and even its gall known as a robin's pin-cushion was used to check haemorrhaging. This strange green and scarlet, mossy growth was also placed under the pillow of an insomniac to bring restful sleep.

The plant has a multitude of colloquial names. Those favoured in Gloucestershire being "Hip-tree" (still in use), "Hip-rose" and "Hedge-Speaks".

The Lowly Bramble

Almost every hedgerow in the country, somewhere along its length, boasts a clump of brambles. The luscious fruit hangs shining in the early Autumn sunshine and even yet tempts town dwellers out into the lanes to gather a free harvest. It appears to be one of the few offerings of the countryside still recognized and collected even by those who claim to know nothing of country matters.

Nowadays it is mainly used for pie fillings, jam making, or perhaps wine making, but these represent only a few of its former uses. In fact, the fruit was perhaps less used than other parts of the plant. Medicinally the bark of the root and the leaves were widely used as an astringent. It was even thought that young shoots eaten as a salad helped to cement loose teeth. Both the flowers and fruit were traditionally used to cure snake bites, while the whole plant was considered a charm against all sorts of disorders and spells! Perhaps surprisingly, old herbalists considered its fruit would stop looseness of the bowels, and, more credibly, sooth sore throats and mouths.

The plant puts out long tendrils which, unless they gain support from an underlying shrub, are not strong enough to support their own weight. Consequently, they bend down and reroot where they touch the ground to form arching loops. These, in Gloucestershire, were greatly sought after as it was believed that by passing an afflicted child backwards and forwards through the arching plant, he could be cured of a hernia or rupture. Similarly, by passing the child three times through the loops on three consecutive mornings, whooping cough could be remedied.

Besides medicinal uses, the bramble was in great demand on the farm. Its long, pliable shoots made an excellent rope. Occasionally, the cut tendrils were drawn through a ring to remove the thorns, making the handling of the resulting binding material less damaging to the hands. In this form it was widely used on Cotswold farms for binding the corn sheaves at harvest, and also for securing the thatch applied to a hayrick to prevent it from being blown away in the winds of winter.

Probably the thorns were not removed when the bramble tendrils were incorporated in turfs placed on a fresh grave. They spiked into the root mass and the ends of the tendrils were trampled into the surrounding grass where they quickly rooted to bind the old and new into a uniform sod. Any brambles which grew could be cut back when the grave was next "tidied".

Brambles also found a place in the home, where their flexible runners were used to bind straw matting, and in the orchards to make bee skeps. These could either be straw bound with brambles, or if the bramble prickles were removed, then could be of the briars alone.

Although the fruit can look very tempting during a mild October, still apparently juicy and ripe, a careful watch should be kept on the calendar, for after 10th October (Michaelmas on the old calendar), the Devil puts his mark on all the remaining fruit.

In the Forest of Dean, to "mooche blackberries" or even more simply to "mooche" was to go blackberry picking, and the following is a recipe which can be followed after a successful mooching expedition.

47

Blackberry Vinegar

Gather the berries on a dry day and place them in an earthenware vessel. Cover with malt vinegar and allow them to stand for three days to draw out the juice. Strain, leaving the mixture to drip all day. Measure the resulting liquid and add 1lb sugar to each pint. Boil gently for 5 minutes in a preserving pan removing any scum which forms. When cool, bottle and cork.

This can be kept till winter when it forms a remedy for feverish colds. A teaspoon when diluted with water will quench the thirst then other drinks fail to do so.

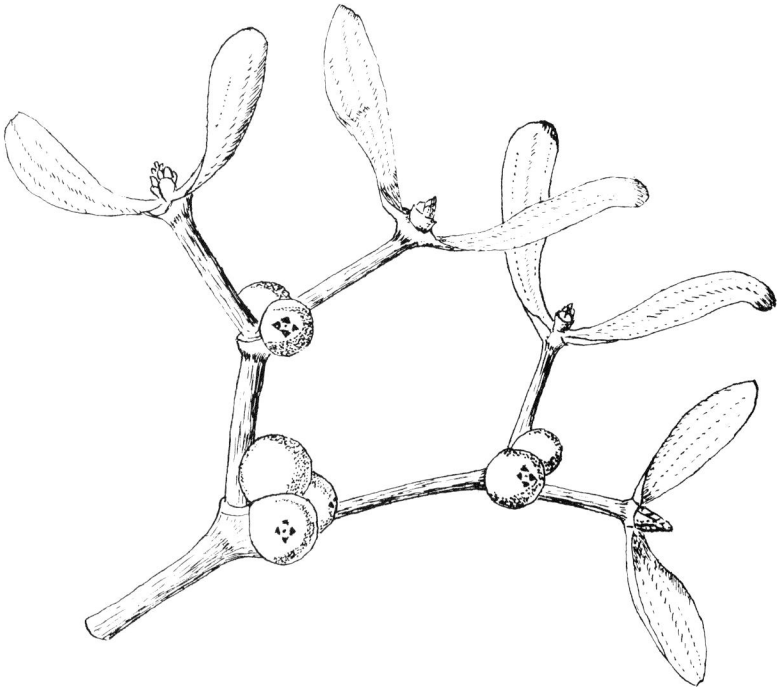

The Kissing Bough

Mistletoe is one of Gloucestershire's specialities, probably occurring more frequently here than in any other county. It is a plant which thrives in the Severn Vale and the Wye Valley, with only rare occurrences on the Cotswold plateau.

The plant is parasitic and grows well on trees and shrubs in the open, such as in orchards or parkland. Rarely is it to be found in woodland except occasionally in planted poplar groves. It favours apple, hawthorn, lime, poplar, willow and pear.

Very occasionally it grows on oak, and when doing so, in times past, was highly prized by the Druids, supposedly being cut ceremoniously by a white-robed priest with a golden sickle. An old hedgerow oak at Frampton-on-Severn is the only example in Gloucestershire of mistletoe growing on oak.

According to Norse mythology, Balder, the God of Peace, was killed by an arrow of mistletoe wood. At the request of the other gods, life was restored to him. Subsequently, the plant was put in the care of the Goddess of Love who ordained that everyone passing beneath it should receive a kiss. Hence the origin of our custom of kissing beneath the mistletoe.

The plant is mainly spread by birds, in particular the mistle thrush which greedily devours the berries, each consisting of a single seed embedded in a sweet pulp. It is the stickiness of this flesh which makes the bird wipe its beak on a nearby branch, thus transferring the seed to a new host.

The adhesive qualities of the berry have led to one of the plant's cruellest uses — the manufacture of bird lime. This is a glue-like mixture containing tempting bait, once used to lure thousands of small birds, especially finches, to a lifetime of captivity.

A Sting in the Tail

Much maligned is the stinging nettle, or ettle as it was known locally. Gardeners rip it out by the yard while land owners slash down extensive beds of this plant. Yet during the years of the Second World War, its value was recognized and people all over the country picked it in quantity. In 1942, the County Herb Committees were each requested to collect 100 tons of it. The target was not quite reached, but that which was gathered was used to extract a dark-green dye essential for war-time camouflage.

The plant loves a nitrogen-rich soil and consequently its presence often indicates an ancient settlement. For example, near Elkstone, the site of a derelict shepherd's hut is marked by an extensive patch of nettles. This would be a good spot to come in Spring to collect the young tops of the plant which has been used by countryfolk for generations as a spinach-like vegetable.

Legend claims that the plant was introduced by the Romans to serve a dual purpose. Firstly it was used as the basis for nettle beer, a drink much revered at latin-style orgies. Secondly, a bunch of it was supposedly used as a whip for stimulating the skin to produce a warming rash, much welcome to those used to the warmth of Mediterranean sun in the cold climate of Gloucestershire.

Later settlers in the county employed it in a more gentle fashion, brewing from its leaves a tea surprisingly used to relieve nettle rash, but also to cure rheumatism, sore throats, bronchitis and asthma. A more violent cure for severe rheumatism was to thrash the affected part of the body with a bunch of nettles.

Of course, one of the well known effects of the nettle is its sting, and one of the equally well-known cures is rubbing with a dock leaf. In the vicinity of Cranham this was accompanied by the chanting of the following verse;

> "Nettle in, dock out,
> Dock out, nettle in.
> Dock rub nettle out;
> Dick, dock, stinging nettle,
> Never let blood settle."

Despite the trauma of being stung by a nettle, its effects are not long-lasting, giving rise to the Gloucestershire saying of "It is better to be stung by a nettle than pricked by a rose."

Substitute Tobacco

Old Man's Beard, Traveller's Joy, Gypsy's Baccy —three evocative names for the wild clematis, a plant which scrambles along our Cotswold lanes throughout the year.

In early summer, the plant is covered with small green and white flowers, but these pale into insignificance when compared to its early autumn display of fluffy white seed heads. As winter approaches, the freshness fades and, as the seeds begin to fall, they get caught up in the surrounding hedges — a grey, cobwebby mat which gives rise to the name "Old Man's Beard".

When fresh, all parts of the plant are poisonous, but on drying, its chemical composition can be changed to render it a good cattle fodder.

Man has found all sorts of strange uses for the plant. Its long, flexible stems have been used to bind faggots or thatch, and it has been woven into baskets and beehives. Perhaps the oddest use was as a cigarette. It was found that if the dried stalks were cut up into short lengths, they could be ignited and would draw well without bursting into flames.

Supposedly, the flavour resembled that of tobacco. It is from this use that the name "Gypsy's Baccy" is derived together with two other variants on the same theme — "Shepherd's Delight" and "Poor Man's Friend".

The Flower of The Forest

Fairy Caps, Snaupers, Snoxums and Snompers — all local names bestowed upon the elegant tall spires of the foxglove. It thrives on the sandy soils of the Forest of Dean, its distribution mirroring the underlying geological pattern of sandstones. Not only does it provide a blaze of colour throughout the summer months, but also a rich supply of food for the humble bees who often fill the woodland glades with a load humming as they climb round inside the bell-shaped blooms in search of honey. Indeed, a visiting preacher to the area who gave a long, dull sermon was once described as "a-buz'n away like a dumbley dory in a snoxum."

The individual flowers also gave great delight to local children who would blow into the bell of the flower to inflate it before banging it as a city child might burst a paper bag.

To adults, the flowers served a more useful purpose, as the leaves when boiled up produced a disinfectant. A wash of this concoction over the walls of a house got rid of earwigs, woodlice and other insect infestations.

Even the Forest dogs were washed in the brew if they became flea-ridden or showed any signs of mange.

The World's Smallest Nature Reserve

Ranunculus ophioglossifolius is rather a complicated name for a small member of the buttercup family — in English known as adder's tongue spearwort, and locally by the affectionate name of the Badgeworth buttercup.

It was first identified in Gloucestershire in 1890, and soon it was realized what a rarity was growing in the county.

The spot where the spearwort was found was adjacent the Badgeworth to Up Hatherley Road on the banks of a stock pool used by both cattle and horses until 1933. Development threatened the site in 1932, but fortunately one of the editors of the original "Flora of Gloucestershire" stepped in and bought the land which he subsequently presented to the Society for the Preservation of Nature Reserves.

The management of the site for the next thirty years was in the care of the Cotteswold Naturalists' Field Club, until 1962, when it was handed over to the newly formed Gloucestershire Trust for Nature Conservation (GTNC).

Today, the reserve comprises 346 square yards of land including a small marsh and part of the original pool. The number of flowering plants varies from year to year, depending on the weather, particularly in the preceding Autumn when germination occurs, and on the wetness of the marsh. Up to a thousand plants have been known to bloom in a good season.

Hopefully, the future of this plant is now secured and it will continue to flower in the county for many years to come on what is possibly the world's smallest nature reserve.

Spring

"The delicate lavender-hued lady's smock, white hedge garlic, starry stitchwort, blue bugle, yellow spotted hempnettle, and azure germander speedwell decked the gown of spring with living jewels; and from a faint violet-tinted waving mowing field came the exquisite scent of vernal grass."

A Wanderer's Gleanings
John A. Farmer (1927)

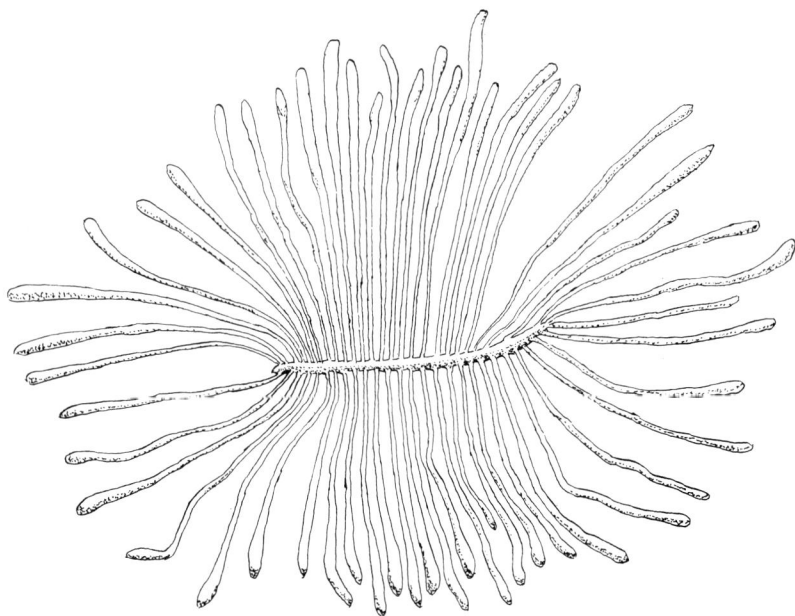

The Elm — An English Institution

In the middle years of the present century, the elm was an integral part of the English countryside. Its stately crowns added to the beauty of almost every hedgerow, its silhouette recognizable as an integral part of the Gloucestershire landscape.

The elm was especially at home in the Severn Vale, although it also grew up on the rather poorer soils of the Cotswolds. Numerous village cricket grounds and churchyards sheltered in its towering shade.

Rarely was it found in woodlands, preferring the open aspect of agricultural land where each tree could grow freely with little interference from overshadowing neighbours.

But, in the early years of the 1970s, tragedy struck in the form of a fungal disease carried by a beetle rejoicing in the latin name of Scolytus scolytus. The first sign of the disease is drooping of shoots and yellowing of leaves, initially on one branch which dies within a few weeks, the whole tree succumbing within a short time.

54

The beetle breeds under the bark of recently dead elm trees. The female burrows under the bark where the male prepares a nuptual chamber. After mating has taken place, the female moves between the bark and sapwood of the tree, laying a string of eggs alternately on opposite sides of the chamber. On hatching, the grubs begin to feed and tunnel at right-angles to the main chamber, leaving an immediately recognizable radiating pattern of galleries.

After hatching, the young beetles emerge through circular holes and fly to other, living elms where they feed on sap, obtained largely from the growing tips of living elms. The beetles invariably carry with them the fungus which infects the tree, thereby assuring future breeding sites.

The infection, known as Dutch Elm Disease, raged through the North American continent in the 1960s, reaching Britain some time before 1970. By 1973, over 50% of Gloucestershire elms were dead or dying, and by 1976, 92% had yielded to the dreaded disease.

Despite the ravages of Dutch Elm Disease, the elm is not lost for ever from our countryside. Suckers from the roots of affected trees are sprouting vigorously in our hedges. If they grow to a mature tree, they are again affected by the fungus, but it seems that the host beetle does not favour shrubs and so the modern elm survives as a hedgerow constituent as opposed to a standard tree.

Food from the Wild

"Yeaver yeard tell on pignuts, mister?" he resumed. "Thaay be good ter eat, an' oi knows where some on um bides."
"Do you?" I said.
"Ai, thaay looks just' like humbrella's t'wrong way roun' — only smaller," he informed me in a most confidential tone of voice. "Us digs up t'roots; thaay be t'pignuts an' be good to eat."

A Wanderer's Gleaning
John A. Farmer (1927)

Tisty-Tosty

This strange Gloucestershire name, and also a simpler version — tosty, was given to the cowslip. It was derived from the ball which was made from the flower heads presumably for tossing into the air.

The balls were each made from fifty or sixty flower heads which were tied onto a string. During the making, the string was stretched between two chairs or trees and the heads tied at closely spaced intervals along it. The ends of the string were released and the flowers bunched closely together with their open bell-like florets pointing outwards to form the ball. The two ends of the string were finally tied to hold the finished article firmly.

The flowers were also favourites of the flower sellers who would gather armfuls from the Gloucestershire fields to offer them for sale in the nearby big towns and cities.

> "In the city's busy streets,
> By rich men's doors,
> On whose white steps
> The flower girl sets her stores,
> In wicker basket
> Grouped to lure the sight,
> They stop and tempt
> Full many a wistful wight."

Besides being picked for their decorative value, cowslips were also gathered in their thousands for medicinal purposes. Cowslip wine (taken with a little water) was considered excellent for giddiness caused by nervous debility or excitement, ánd would also cure trembling. In old herbals, the root was called Radix arthritica as it was used to cure muscular rheumatism. Some people drank cowslip water to aid the memory while the crushed flowers were used to remove spots, freckles and wrinkles from the face.

Alexander Pope, the famous poet and a frequent visitor to the Bathurst Estate at Cirencester Park, wrote in a letter:-

> "For the future, I'll drown all high thoughts in the Lethe of Cowslip Wine."

He obviously was familiar with its soporific properties!

The hanging configuration of the flower heads suggested to our ancestors a bunch of keys — the emblem of St. Peter. One legend relates that St. Peter dropped his keys when he heard that a duplicate of the key of Heaven had been made. Everywhere on earth where they landed, a cowslip sprang up.

Largely because of over-picking, but also due to changes in agricultural practices, cowslip numbers declined rapidly in the middle years of the present century. Fortunately, because of prompt legislation which made it a protected species, the cowslip has staged a revival and, although not now present in its former numbers, it can be enjoyed as a visual spectacle in many fields of the county.

Enigmatic Elder

No tree seems to inspire such ambivalent emotions as the elder (or ellan as it is called locally). It grows very rapidly and openly so seems to have little use in forming a dense, stockproof hedge. Yet in 1675, in "Mystery of Husbandry", Worlidge wrote:-

> "A considerable fence may be made of Elder, set of reasonable hasty Truncheons, like the Willow and may be laid with great curiosity: this makes a speedy shelter for a garden from Winds, Beasts and such-like injuries."

Supposedly, posts made of elder last in the ground longer than the same sized iron bar. This gave rise to the old saying:-

> "An eldern stake and a blackthorn ether (hedge)
> Will make a hedge last for ever."

— surely a much more successful way of using elder in making a hedge.

The elder gives rise to a wealth of legend. It is supposedly the tree on which Judas hung himself, and also provided the wood for the Cross of Calvary.

Religion and heathen superstition become so mixed in the beliefs concerning this tree that it is difficult to separate the origins of the many strange customs associated with it. Certainly no self-respecting Gloucestershire man would ever make a cradle from its wood, as a child laid in such a bed would get no rest.

Conversely, an elder tree planted in the garden was said to drive away evil spirits. Related to this, a cross made of two twigs of the elder, hung over a stable door, protected the animals from witches and their spells.

The wood of the elder was much honoured and few countrymen would burn it. The following extract is taken from "Notes on Certain Superstitions in the Vale of Gloucester".

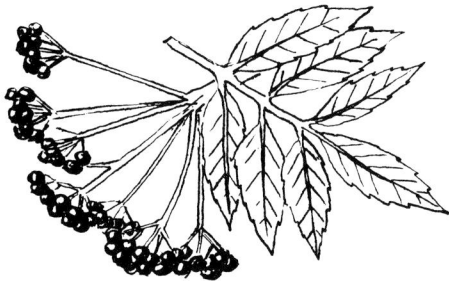

"Some men were employed in removing an old hedgerow, partially formed of Elder trees. They had bound up all the other wood into faggots for burning, but had set apart the Elder and enquired of their master how it was to be disposed of. Upon his saying that he should of course burn it with the rest, one of the men said with an air of undisguised alarm, that he had never heard of such a thing as burning Ellan wood, and, in fact, so strongly did he feel upon the subject, that he refused to participate in the act of tying it up."

All parts of the trees found either culinary, medicinal or cosmetic use. John Evelyn, writing of the elder, says:-

"If the medicinal properties of its leaves, bark and berries were fully known, I cannot tell what our countryman could ail for which he might not fetch a remedy from every hedge, either for sickness or wounds."

An excellent wine can be made from the flowers and berries, jam from the berries and an insect repellent from the leaves.

According to local usage, rheumatism sufferers should always carry a cross made from a small piece of elder wood cut from a young shoot just above and below a joint to leave the buds projecting at each side giving the cruciform shape. This is especially efficacious if the elder from which the wood is obtained grows in a churchyard.

For Sale — In Cheltenham Market

Along the hedges the spindlewood still kept its leaves, and the bright pink sheaths had not yet split open to show the bright orange berries within. I am always glad to find spindle growing in secluded spots, for it is one of the bushes which the gypsies ravage to sell great branches of it in Cheltenham. It is a brittle wood, never making a big tree, and one frequently finds a whole clump smashed and splintered till little more than stumps remain of the trees that were once grown to make spindles for the looms and skewers.

Margaret Westerling (1939)
from "County Contentments"

59

The Yew — Fact and Fantasy

Appropriately designated the tree of immortality, it is difficult to imagine that a mature yew was ever young. Gracing most Gloucestershire churchyards, the yew has a furrowed trunk supporting wide-spread boughs densely covered with foliage to give a deep shade and form an excellent wind-break.

Unfortunately, its fruit is poisonous both to man and farm animals. It was therefore unsuitable for planting in pasture land. Consequently, the cottage garden and churchyard became its home, and here the yew flourished for centuries before attaining a size suitable for its most famed use — to provide wood for bows.

For this purpose, the wood was preferably of uniform colour, the best bows being made from the bole as the boughs were too knotty. According to a statute of Edward IV, every Englishman was ordered to possess a bow as tall as himself made of yew, wych-hazel or laburnum.

Bows were the mainstay of English armies and it is reported that after an affray at Cirencester during the reign of Henry IV, eighty archers of the town, including a number of women, were thanked for their services.

Perhaps the most famous yews in Gloucestershire are those which grace Painswick churchyard. Most of the existing trees were planted about three hundred years ago, legend relating that there are only ninety-nine of them and can never be more. If an attempt is made to increase this number, either some of the older trees will die, or the new ones will fail to grow. However, various estimates have claimed that up to 118 yews have been established at one time.

Nowadays, the yew-lined paths at Painswick are merely used as a short cut between two busy streets but, in earlier times, the churchyard was quite a fashionable spot to be seen, for Rudder states that it was "the place of resort for the ladies and polite inhabitants of the town in fair weather."

Holy Herb

The word sainfoin is derived from the French Sainte-foin meaning holy hay, a title given to this plant which, by reputation, shares the honours with lady's bedstraw as having been the plant chosen to line the manger in Bethlehem to keep the infant Jesus warm. Legend relates that as the baby was laid in the crib, the plant burst into flower so that he was surrounded by a halo of bright flowers.

Indeed, the colourful pink flowering spikes which grace our waysides during the long days of midsummer, have a striking appearance. They particularly favour a limey soil and at one time were grown extensively on Cotswold farms, supposedly introduced into this country as an agricultural crop about three centuries ago by the squire of Daylesford, a village situated in the north-eastern corner of Gloucestershire.

The plant can develop an extensive root system and so can obtain moisture from deep underground in periods of drought. In some quarries, where sections through the ground can be seen, the roots have been observed up to a depth of twenty feet.

It was used either as pasturage or for making into hay, and was a good crop for very dry land unsuitable for normal arable crops, and which would yield little produce if laid down to pasture.

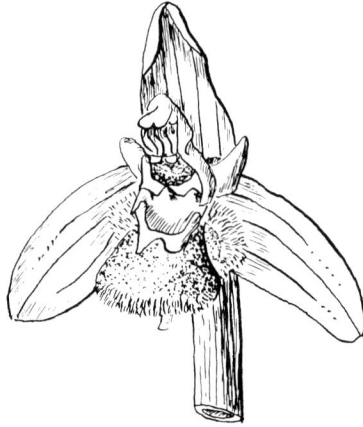

Orchid Specials

No flowers arouse more interest than the orchid family. Their variety of form and rarity all add to the excitement when one of them suddenly impinges on the scene. From the first of the season — the appropriately-named early purple orchis — through to the rare autumn ladies' tresses, they add zest to the Gloucestershire flowering season.

Although not many species of orchids occur in this country, world-wide, there are more orchid species than grasses. Approximately thirty species can be found in the county, including some, such as the fly orchid, only pollinated by one type of insect. The plants produce a scent to attract the specific insects which then attempt to mate with the suitably shaped flower, in the process collecting the pollinia, sticky sacks of pollen, which are subsequently carried to another flower to ensure cross-pollination.

As it says in "The Flora and Fauna of Gloucestershire", published in 1892:-

> "Perhaps there is no wild flower that so much delights the botanical rambler as the orchid. We well remember the rapture with which we first happened on a clump of O.apifera (bee orchid), at Crickley. The sun was hot, and the road hither from Cheltenham dusty and tiresome, but all fatigue was forgotten, when this mimicry of active bee life came to view."

62

A Flowery Verge

"Celandines vied with dandelions in tinting the grassy margin
of the road with their sun-kissed blossoms, and, where short
cutting had been made to drain the surface water into the
ditches, a few pale faces of modest shepherd's purse peeped.
Occasionally the fringed flower of a coltsfoot stood out on its
sturdy stem, and, here and there, the pale blue speedwell could
be seen nestling on a hedge bank."

A Wanderer's Gleanings
John A. Farmer (1927)

Stone Walls

To a botanist, a drystone wall may seem a poor substitute for that
haven of wild-life, the hedgerow. Yet, they provide shelter, and, under
their protection, many plant species thrive as evidenced by the following
lines written in 1908:-

"Grass banks are piled up against the base of them, thick in
flowers, poppy, scabious, cranesbill, cow-parsnip, campion,
bedstraw, each in its season."

The Cotswolds
F.R.G. Duckworth

A Little Bunch of Primroses

"Here was further assurance that the growth of the year had
continued, for I was able to pick a little bunch of primroses,
no longer an isolated bud or two, which was all I could find a
short time before. They had the earthy freshness of the early
spring flowers, a delicacy of smell lost to the later wealth of
blossom, for all its fragrance."

Country Contentments
Margaret Westerling (1939)

Blue Violets

"The churchyard this morning is perfumed with blue violets; I
gathered a bunch of them and continued my journey to Hinchwick."

Highways and Byways in Oxford & The Cotswolds
H. A. Evans (1905)

63

Simpler's Joy

Vervain is a plant which in recent years has lost much of its former popularity. At one time, it was a plant known by everyone as it had so many uses, both medicinal and in witchcraft. The Druids held the plant in special reverence, although the great herbalist — Gerard — wrote in his Herbal:

> "Manie old wives fables are written of vervayne tending to witchcraft and sorcerie, which you may read elsewhere, for I am not willing to trouble your care with such trifles."

Rarely is the plant found except in the vicinity of human settlement. It occurs, in apparently remote countryside, at a particular spot in the Slad Valley, but research shows that it is actually growing adjacent the site of a long derelict shop.

According to Knapp, writing in the Severn Vale in 1829, it was then more common than it is nowadays. The following is an extract from his diary:

> "The plain, simple, unadorned vervain (verbena officinalis), is one of our most common, and decidedly waste-loving plants. Disinclined to all cultured places, it fixes its residence by waysides, and old stone quarries, thriving under the feet of every passing creature. The celebrity that this plant obtained in very remote times, without its possessing one apparent quality, or presenting by its manner of growth, or form, any mysterious character to arrest the attention, or excite imagination, is very extraordinary, and perhaps unaccountable: most nations venerated, esteemed, and used it; the ancients had their Verbenalia, at which period the temples and frequented places were strewed and sanctified with vervain; the beasts for sacrifice and the altars were verbenated, the one filleted, the other strewed with the sacred herb; no incantation or lustration was perfect without the aid of this plant."

Certainly, our Gloucestershire ancestors used it as one of the herbs which they tied over doorways to deter witches on festivals such as Mid-summer's Eve, and for thirty listed medicinal purposes, hence one of its country names — simpler's joy.

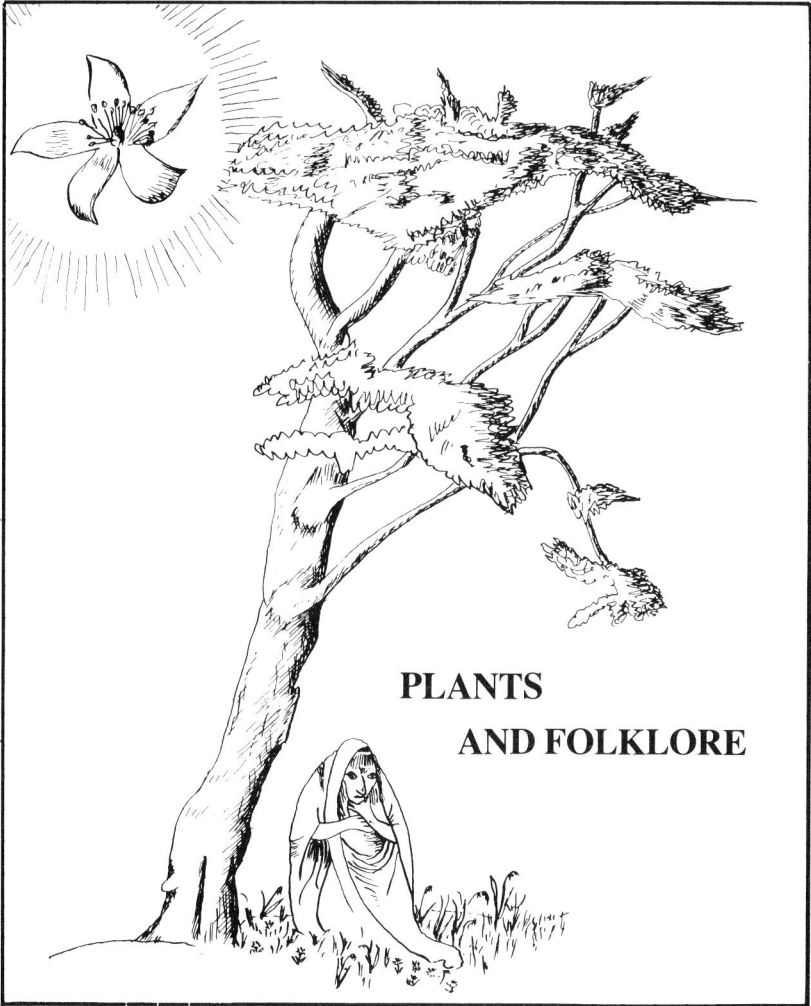

PLANTS
AND FOLKLORE

The Pear Trees

Anyone searching nowadays for local folk tales must generally go to old books and notes as the art of story telling is sadly a dying craft. However, the following story was heard in a pub in Charlton Kings during the 1980s.

The fruit hung large and juicy, tempting the traveller to stretch up and pick the ripe pears.

"Strange" he thought. "Why should five such beautiful fruit trees be growing in a hedge? They are worthy specimens to grace any orchard."

The man continued along the road towards Gloucester but stopped in the next village at the inn. He ordered a drink and then, the bar being empty, engaged the landlord in conversation.

"Those are fine pear trees growing in the hedge up the road towards Tewkesbury."

"Yes," replied the landlord. "They once grew in an orchard near Evesham, an area renowned for the quality of its fruit. Unfortunately, the young trees were near some old, tall elms, the home of several crows. No sooner was the first crop ripe on those trees, than down came the black terrors to gorge themselves on the luscious fruit."

"The same thing happened year after year. Before the farmer ever had chance to harvest the pears, they had disappeared down the gullets of the crows. At last, he decided something must be done about the thefts and so, just as the fruit was ripening, he painted the branches thickly with birdlime. Sure enough, a few days later, when the fruit was at its peak, down flew the birds and landed in the trees."

"There was such a squawking and flapping as the crows tried to move their feet, but all in vain, for the more they struggled, the faster they became stuck. The farmer was delighted that his plan had worked. "I'll go and get my gun," he said aloud, " . . . and get rid of those pests once and for all."

"The crows heard the threat and flapped their wings so vigorously that they pulled the trees up by their roots. They flew off with them, their only idea being to put as great a distance as possible between themselves and the angry farmer."

"After a while it started raining and gradually the bird lime was washed from the branches until at last the trees fell from the birds' grasp and landed in the hedge where you saw them."

The traveller finished his drink, nodded to his host and went on his way, calling back over his shoulder, "Worcestershire's loss was Gloucestershire's gain. I've never seen such fine trees."

St. Augustine's Oak

According to the writings of the Venerable Bede, in the seventh century St. Augustine journeyed westwards from Canterbury to a place appropriately called St. Augustine's Oak. Here, by arrangement, he met with the bishops of the Celtic Church to discuss how the Word of God could be spread to the disbelievers in these islands.

The precise location of this conference is not known, although according to Bede's manuscript, it was situated on the borders of the Forest of Dean by the River Severn and was under an oak tree.

Although there are several claimants to the site, perhaps the strongest of these is that of the village of Broad Oak. Geographically it fits the description, while its very name indicates the existence of a tree of the correct species of considerable fame. Additionally, it lay on the Roman road running between Gloucester and Caerleon in South Wales so would have been accessible to both parties. Moreover, in the neighbourhood there is a field which still bears the name "Stroods", an old Danish word meaning meeting place.

The Angel's Message

A plant which loves the unimproved limestone pastures of the Cotswolds is the carline thistle. Unlike other British thistles, the principal colour of its flower head is a straw yellow with a desiccated appearance reminiscent of everlasting flowers beloved by flower arrangers.

On the approach of damp weather the outer bracts partially close up to protect the inner part of the flower from moisture, a mechanism that still functions after picking. It was for this reason that in times past, the plant was gathered and hung over cottage doors to forecast coming rain.

Legend relates that the name is merely a corruption of Charlemagne's Thistle, the plant having been dedicated to the great emperor after his army was decimated by a dreadful pestilence. All known medicines seemed useless and so Charlemagne prayed for divine help. In a dream, an angel fired a bolt from a cross-bow into the air, telling the emperor to note on which plant it landed. This plant possessed wonderful healing properties and would restore his men to health. The plant miraculously pointed out was a little yellow thistle known ever since as Charlemagne's or carline thistle.

Spilt Blood

Mary Jones, daughter of Mr. Roynon Jones, lived at Nass, near Lydney. She was murdered in a field adjacent the churchyard, where, it was said, no grass ever grew again.

A Good Threshing

It used to be the custom to place loose straw in front of the door of any man who was known to beat his wife. Supposedly, the loose straw indicated to his neighbours that he had been "threshing".

Maud's Elm

Every week, Maud Bowen journeyed from her home in Swindon village to Cheltenham market, carrying with her the yarn that she and her mother, Margaret, had spun during the week. Hopefully, she returned bearing sufficient money to tide them over another seven days.

It was on one of these journeys that tragedy struck. Maud did not return home in the evening, and the next day her body was found by some villagers in a neighbouring stream. To add to the mystery, the body of her uncle was also discovered nearby, his fingers clasped around a torn piece of Maud's dress.

On investigation of the sad affair, a coroner appointed by the Lord of the Manor, declared that Maud had killed her uncle and subsequently drowned herself, although he could offer no reason for these events.

The body of a person who had committed suicide could not be buried in consecrated ground, and therefore Maud's body was laid to rest at a cross-roads just outside the village. As a further indignity, an elm stake was thrust through her heart to pin her spirit within her body and prevent it from wandering.

After Maud's death, the Lord of the Manor evicted Margaret from the cottage which she had shared with her daughter on the pretext that she alone could not spin sufficient yarn to pay the rent. None of the villagers knew where Margaret went to live but occasionally she would be seen keeping a silent vigil at Maud's grave. The mourning mother never failed to believe in her daughter's innocence.

One day, as she was offering up a silent prayer at the centre of the cross-roads, a grand procession approached — a line of carriages whose coachmen were not pleased to be forced to a standstill by the kneeling woman. The window of the leading carriage opened and, who should lean out, but the Lord of the Manor. The procession was on its way to Bishop's Cleeve Church for the christening of his infant son.

On seeing Margaret, he sent one of his footmen to order her to move. Although the servant came right up to Margaret, she seemed quite oblivious of his presence, and so he put out his hand to her. As he did so, an arrow flew through the air and the unfortunate man fell to the ground, dead, the arrow having entering his brain through his eye.

A flush of anger suffused the face of the Lord of the Manor as he barked out commands to his remaining servants. They scurried in all directions seeking out the bowman, but none could be found. So Margaret, who seemed to be in a daze, was seized and taken to Gloucester Gaol where she was tried and found guilty of witchcraft.

In those days, the savage punishment for practising the Black Arts, was death by burning. The judge deemed it appropriate that Margaret's funeral pyre should be raised at a place where her supposed last act of witchcraft had been perpetrated — at they very spot where her daughter was buried.

The air hung heavy and the birds were silent as poor Margaret was bound to the stake. Brand bearers stepped forward and applied a light to the kindling. The flames snatched at the thin twigs and leapt upwards licking around the base of the thicker logs. Margaret stood, a lone figure, as yet untouched by the flames, completely silent, bearing the ordeal with dignity. Over the crackling of the still infant fire, the voice of the Lord of the Manor boomed, "Confess. Admit that you are a witch." Throughout her trial, Margaret had hotly denied this charge. He harangued her further. "Confess now and Heavenly forgiveness will be yours."

Margaret still said nothing and the watching crowd fell silent waiting for her screams to begin. Suddenly the silence was broken by a tremendous thunderclap which seemed to shake the very foundations of the earth. The faggots forming the pyre vibrated and collapsed, producing dense clouds of smoke and extinguishing the flames. The smoke enveloped everyone and it was several minutes before it had cleared sufficiently for someone to notice that Margaret had vanished, and that on the ground lay the body of the Lord of the Manor, yet another victim of an arrow.

Many years later, the truth of this story was told by an old man called Walter. In his youth, he had been betrothed to Maud, and on the fateful day when she had died, he had set out to meet her coming home from market. As he approached the bridge, he had heard Maud's scream when she was accosted by two men, namely the Lord of the Manor and her own uncle. As they attacked her, she had let out the scream and Walter had rushed forward. He always carried his bow and a supply of arrows with him, and quickly he let fly an arrow which had hit Maud's uncle.

This created a diversion which had allowed Maud to run off, but unfortunately, she had caught her foot against a stone and tumbled into the stream. The Lord of the Manor chased Walter whose fleetness of foot had allowed him to escape. However, by the time he returned to the water, Maud was beyond earthly help.

He left the village in despair and went to live at Hayden. When Margaret was evicted from her cottage, it was to him she had turned for help. He took her into his home, and secretly accompanied her every time she went to visit her daughter's grave. He was the mysterious bowman who had killed the footman. It was also Walter who had shot the Lord of the Manor when the opportune thunderclap diverted attention for a short while during the attempted burning of Margaret.

After Margaret's escape, she had again lived with Walter who had cared for her as if she were his own mother, until her death several years later. He eventually returned to the village of Swindon and managed to rent the very cottage which had once been occupied by Maud and Margaret. He lived there with his memories, and was fascinated watching the growth of an elm tree from the grave of his beloved Maud. This had sprouted from the green elm stake which had been used to pierce her heart. It produced shady branches which for years sheltered her grave from the hot sun of summer and the lashing rains of winter.

The truth of this story cannot be verified, but it is a fact that a tree known as Maud's Elm stood at the cross-roads just outside Swindon village until it was struck by lightning in 1907 after which it was finally felled, having been declared unsafe.

How Does Your Garden Grow?

"Missus be Master" of a house where sage, rosemary or lavender thrive in the garden.

It is unlucky to transplant flowers from the garden of a ruined house.

Root crops must be planted during a waning moon.
Top crops must be planted during a waxing moon.

Twelfth of May, Stow Fair Day,
Sow your kidney beans today.

Spring cabbages should be planted on Lechlade Fair Day (9th September).

A hawthorn twig stuck into a seed bed will nullify any witches' spells.

Apple Lore

St. Briavels was the centre for a winter custom which survived until the latter years of the last century. This was the exchange of New Year Gift Apples. They consisted of an apple mounted on three legs and trimmed with a nut and a sprig of yew or box. The three parts supposedly represented Sweetness, Fertility and Immortality. Right in the south-west corner of the county and across the River Wye into the adjoining county of Gwent at Chepstow, these decorated apples were known as Monties. One would be carried round from house to house by children chanting:-

> "Monty, Monty, Happy New Year,
> A pocketful of money and cellar full of beer."

The same triple symbolism occurred in the ball-flowers sold to the parishioners of Newnham for three pennies, the money going towards the construction of the reredos in the church. Ball-flowers were popular decorations from the fourteenth century onwards. They consisted of a three-petalled bud supposed to represent that of an apple, although in reality — apple blossom has five petals!

The parish of Awre is enclosed by a broad sweep of the River Severn and is an area famed both for flooding and the growing of apples. Legend relates how a nearby town called Pomerton was drowned beneath the waters of the river. There are no records to show that such a place ever existed but it is thought that, perhaps in one of the periodic shiftings of the course of the river, many of the extensive orchards were submerged and that the story is an allegory indicating that the lost wealth from the fruit was equivalent to the loss of an entire town.

Gourmet's Delight

White Styne, Hagloe-crab, Fox-whelp, Lemon-roy, Cockayne, Hardhead or Kill-boy, and Gilly-flower were all the names of local apples listed by Rudge in 1809.

Our Lady's Little Glass

The delicate flowers of the field bindweed can be found in hedgerows and waste ground throughout Gloucestershire. The gardener may curse its persistence, but its delicate beauty was the reason for its old name of Our Lady's Little Glass. Folk memory recalls the following explanation for such an appellation.

A wagoner was employed to carry casks of wine from the country into the city. He had an enormous cart pulled by six oxen. Normally they travelled the country roads with no difficulty, but one year the rains had been so severe that his beasts could make no headway over the muddy tracks. Eventually, one lunchtime, he could go no further and, as no help was in sight, he rested by the wayside to eat his dinner.

As he sat there, a woman with a baby in her arms, came near and stood watching him with that longing look which said she was starving. The wagoner took pity on the woman and gave her half his food. She thanked him and asked if he could spare a few drops of his wine — not for herself but for her child.

"With pleasure I would give you all the wine I have," replied the man, " . . . but I have no glass to put it in."

The woman went to the hedgerow and plucked a pale pink flower with white stripes shaped exactly like a small glass. He filled it with wine which she offered to the child.

Instantly the sun crept from behind the clouds and effortlessly the oxen pulled the cart free of the mire. When the wagoner looked up to speak to the woman again and offer her a lift, she had vanished. Immediately he knew that the woman to whom he had been speaking was Mary carrying her infant child. Consequently when relating the episode to other travellers he called the flower "Our Lady's Little Glass" —a big name for a small flower.

76

Ash Lore

A few ash boughs thrown into a pond where frogs and toads are present in such numbers as to be a nuisance, will destroy the animals in two or three days.

☆ ☆ ☆

The bark of the ash can be used to cure agues and fevers.

☆ ☆ ☆

The ashes of an ash fire can be used as a poultice to draw blisters.

☆ ☆ ☆

Ash keys when pickled make an excellent sauce which acts as an expeller of venom.

☆ ☆ ☆

If the oak's before the ash,
We shall only have a splash.
But if the ash precedes the oak,
We shall surely have a soak.

☆ ☆ ☆

The tree is one of those capable of curing warts. For each wart take a new pin and push it into the tree. Remove the pin and use it to prick the wart before returning it to the tree. While this is being carried out the following charm should be repeated:-

"Ashen Tree, Ashen Tree,
Pray buy these warts of me."

☆ ☆ ☆

A toothache sufferer can get relief by sitting beneath an ash tree and cutting his toe nails.

Devilish Doings

No large estate was complete without its hazel coppice. Hazel is vigorous in growth and produces new shoots as soon as it is cut down. It is this ability which has rendered it one of man's most useful shrubs. The wood is pliant and tough and is excellent for the making of hurdles, sections of fencing joined together to make temporary fences particularly before Enclosures when there were few hedges or permanent fences.

A team of men would be responsible for cutting a large acreage of hazels and, by the time they had cut the whole area down to stumps, the first cut would again be at a sufficient height for recutting. This cycle varied from seven to fifteen years according to soil and light conditions. The hurdle maker often lived in the woods but in the present century, any surviving hurdle-makers are likely to live in a village to where the raw timber is conveyed.

For the rustic, the hazel provided a free source of food in late summer and autumn. Hazel nuts hang in large clusters, a valuable source of protein provided they can be collected before being gathered and stored as a winter food supply by squirrels.

It was in search of such bounty that a mild sunny day in early October tempted a Minchinhampton man out into the countryside. His wife and family were all at church, but when he was asked to join them, he declared that he would rather walk across the Common.

Approaching a spot known as the Devil's Churchyard, he saw a bunch of hazel nuts hanging temptingly in the hedge. As he stretched up to pick them, he announced triumphantly, "Mine."

A few yards further on, another, even bigger bunch, presented themselves to his gaze.

"Mine," he shouted as he grasped them.

Not much further on, the most magnificent bunch of all caught his eye. As his finger closed on the nuts, a deep voice boomed out, "Mine," and a clawed, hairy hand came out of the bushes and grabbed him.

The man is said to have dropped dead from the shock and his body was buried a few days later in the churchyard, but not before his soul had been taken by the waiting Devil.

Odds and Ends

The blackthorn, being one of the first to flower in spring, was considered a magical tree which drove away any remaining days of winter. However, its blossoms were thought to be unlucky if brought indoors, and it was never worn as a buttonhole.

Picking a bunch of lesser celandines was supposed to encourage cows to give a rich creamy milk. For the same reason, the tuberous roots, which allegedly resembled an udder, were hung in the cowsheds or tied to a cow's tether.

Violets were never brought indoors, as Gloucester folk thought they harboured fleas.

The snowdrop was considered a melancholy flower.

Mary of Painswick

Any child born on a Friday started life with a handicap for he (or she) was destined to be unlucky, and would, in all probability, die either by the hangman's noose or at the hands of a murderer. If this was not bad enough, an unfortunate born on a Good Friday was predestined to bring bad luck to all who came in contact.

This was the threatened fate for a baby girl born to a Painswick woman one Good Friday. The mother knew of all the superstitions and so, immediately after the birth, called in the priest to baptise the child. She also chose the name Mary in honour of the Blessed Virgin, hoping that with divine help, the child might overcome her destiny.

In spite of these precautions, as Mary grew up, she was shunned by everyone in the village. Consequently, she spent many hours roaming the hills alone, walking in the meadows and woods with only the animals and birds for company. She was an observant and inquisitive child and so, in her rambles, learned a good deal about the local herbs.

Reluctantly, people began to come to Mary for help. She used carpenter's herb (now called self-heal) to bind about wounds caused by the slip of a wood-working tool, comfrey to set broken bones and lady smock to ease persistent headaches. Not only did she treat people but also became a skilled animal doctor, always using herbs, love and patience to cure her patients.

Notwithstanding her ability, the Painswick inhabitants could not forget on what day she had been born. The more cures she effected, the more loudly they swore she was a witch, until even her own mother avoided her.

The Manor at Painswick at about this time changed hands, and the new squire was a handsome young man from a nearby village. The locals considered it their duty to warn him of Mary, telling him that there was a Friday-born witch in their midst.

"Who is she?" enquired the young man curiously.

"A young woman who goes by the name of Mary," the people told him. "She poses as an animal doctor."

"Not the Mary who mended my hound's broken leg when I despaired for his life?" he asked.

"Quite possibly, but have nothing more to do with her," warned the villagers.

The squire frowned.

"The life of the whole village, human and animal, depends on skilled herbal practioners like Mary. She is a gifted woman. A knowledge of plants and their uses is a gift from God, not the Devil. Treat her well. If I hear one more word spoken against her, the culprit will be put in the stocks."

With that the story-tellers crept away, and no more tales about Mary were circulated, at least not openly, but it is more difficult to suppress men's thoughts than their words.

Where They Fell!

Beside the busy B4215, about 4 miles north-west of the City of Gloucester, stands a lonely monument. Around it, at the height of summer, masses of meadow cranesbill colour the banks and hedgerows a bluey-purple.

It is said that it was near this spot, during the Civil War, that the Battle of Barber's Bridge was fought. An army of Welshmen was raised by the Duke of Beaufort to attack the city which was in Parliamentarian hands. Reinforcements were expected and so the army entrenched themselves near Highnam to await their colleagues.

News of their arrival reached the city and, before assistance arrived, a Parliamentarian force led by Sir William Waller crossed the River Severn downstream and crept up behind the Royalist encampment while their attention was diverted by skirmishes directed at them from the City. The ensuing battle was bloody and many of the Welshmen were slain.

To this day, the soil in that vicinity and the local River Leadon are very red, a result, so the locals say of the Welsh blood spilt in that battle in 1643. In addition, it is claimed that a cranesbill sprouted from the blood-stained earth at every spot where a Royalist had fallen.

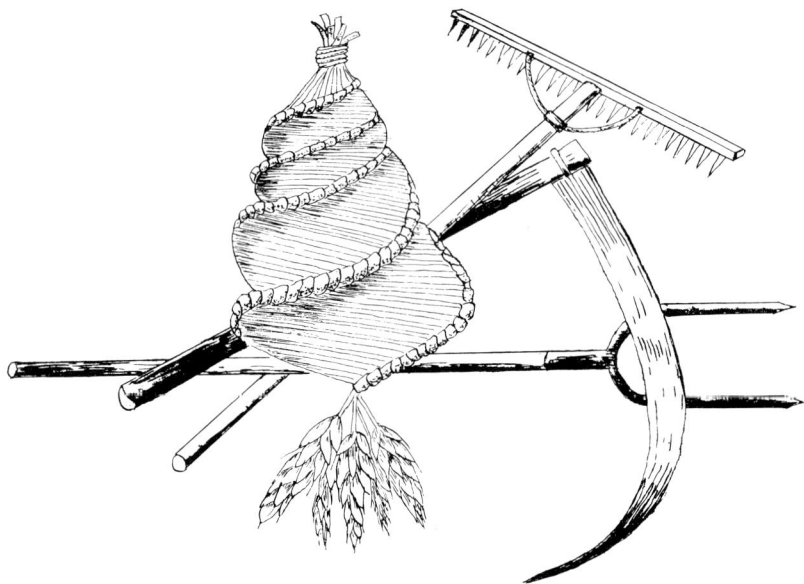

Harvest Home

August 1st or Lammas-tide marked the start of harvesting in the rural calendar. This was derived from the Celtic festival of Lugnasad. When adopted by Christian society, it became the Festival of the First Fruits, the time when the first sheaf of corn was cut, ground and made into a loaf of bread offered in church and dedicated to God.

After this first cut, the harvest got into full swing. Teams of harvesters moved across the fields, swinging in line, a scythe's sweep apart taking their pace from the leader. Some women helped with the cutting — all unnecessary household chores abandoned for the period. Those for whom cutting was too energetic, helped with the stooking and carrying thus earning the right of leazing or gleaning, and a share in the Harvest Home.

Folk believed that the Harvest Spirit dwelt in the fields, and that as the reapers cut, she was forced to move into the ever-decreasing area of standing corn. No-one wanted to destroy her final hiding place, and often the reapers would retreat and take turns to throw their sickles at the last few stalks. When eventually severed these would be made into a Corn Dolly which supposedly represented the Harvest Spirit and would be given pride of place at the Harvest Home supper.

Before that, however, the last load had to be carried home. The children ran beside the wagon singing:

> Up, up, up, up, harvest home
> Carried the last load and never bin throwed."

At the leazing, the day after the last load had been brought in, the church bell was tolled at eight in the morning acting as a signal that folk might go into the fields and glean until only the stubble remained.

This custom was strictly enforced, a fact which once brought trouble to the people of Temple Guiting. They waited for the bell and then rushed to the field called Oak Piece which was on the road to Stow. When they arrived, they found the townsfolk of Stow already occupying the meadow. A pitched battle ensued during the course of which, the Stow invaders were repulsed.

Everyone who had helped in any way in the harvest came to the Harvest Home, a time of celebration at which the farmer fed his work force liberally, and with song and dance, a good time was had by all.

The Corn Dolly hung in the barn throughout the winter, and, the following spring was returned to her rightful place in the fields, being buried as they were ploughed ready for reseeding.

Are You Sitting Comfortably?

A legendary box tree at Hayles Abbey was cut into the shape of a seat. It was here that Cromwell supposedly sat to watch a battle in nearby Winchcombe.

The Glastonbury Thorn

Joseph of Arimathea and eleven companions were the first Christian missionaries to arrive on these shores, landing on the banks of the Bristol Channel. Initially they were not well received and wandered in search of a spot to settle and establish their first mission. The weather was cold and snowy and it was Christmas Eve when they came to a place near Glastonbury. They were so tired that Joseph thrust his stick of hawthorn into the ground and lay down to sleep.

To the amazement of all twelve, on waking in the morning, the stick had taken root, branched and budded — all in the space of a winter's night. But instead of the ordinary white may blossom, the tree bore blooms stained with red. The missionaries immediately recognized this as representing the blood of Christ and realized that it was no ordinary phenomenon but a miracle to show them that this was the place ordained for them to build their first church.

It is said that the tree continued to bloom every year on Christmas Eve and crowds would come to watch the miracle. The tree claimed to be the original thorn at Glastonbury was uprooted by the Puritans but not before many cuttings from it had been spread around the country. There were at least two of these recorded in Gloucestershire. The first was near Gloucester and the other at Pintwell Lodge near Colesbourne. In mild winters, the Pintwell Lodge Thorn, was recorded as blooming around the Christmas season.

All the Threes!

On the wind-swept heights of Cleeve Hill were a clump of stunted beeches known as the Three Sisters. In the Forest of Dean, near to New Fancy Colliery, stood three giant sessile oaks —supposedly remnants of the mediaeval forest — which went under the name of the Three Brothers.

A Powerful Herb

In Gloucestershire villages, parsley wine was much sought after as an aphrodisiac. However, to make plenty of the wine, large quantities of parsley are needed and, as many present-day gardeners know, it is not the easiest of plants to germinate or transplant.

It was said to be a herb of the Devil and, once sown, descended to Hell three times to honour its master before it dared to show its face on the earth. This was the reason that germination took so long. Many cottage gardeners claimed that it was best sown with curses by someone having a bad character. If there was no such person to hand, (and who would admit to such an indictment merely to be given the chore of planting everyone's parsley?), then a good man must do the sowing after returning from church on Good Friday.

If a gardener decided it really was too dificult to grow from seed, then the only other way was to transplant some of a friend's crop. Even this deed was fraught with difficulties, for it was said to be dangerous to transplant parsley and, fatal to be given some as a gift. The only safe possibility was for the donor to point silently to the bed of parsley, and for the recipient to return later when the donor was not around and secretly steal some.

With all these hazards it is surprising that the folk of Gloucestershire did not find a simpler love potion!

Old Recipe for Parsley Wine

Boil 1lb. of parsley in 10 pints of water until it softens. Strain the liquid into a large crock. Add 3lb. sugar, a lump of ginger and 2 sliced lemons. Stir the mixture until the sugar dissolves. Allow to cool and when lukewarm add 1oz. yeast and leave covered with a muslin cloth for 2 weeks. Skim off any floating material and decant the liquid, leaving the thick residue behind. Bottle the wine and leave for at least twelve months before drinking.

Kill or Cure?

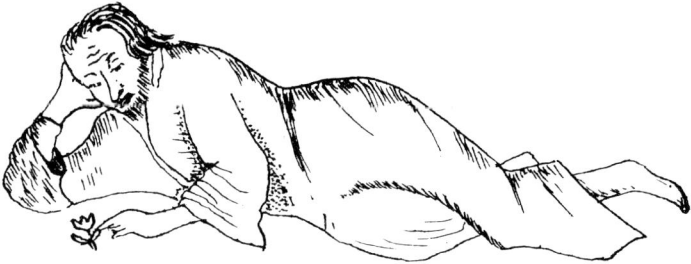

Coughs — These can be eased by feeding the patient a mixture of hyssop, horehound and coltsfoot soaked in linseed oil.

Earache — Relief can be gained by dropping into the ear, juice squeezed from the houseleek.

Rheumatism — This was a common complaint and numerous remedies are recorded.
1. In the Dursley area, a decoction of wood sage was drunk in the spring to prevent rheumatism.
2. Parsley or celery chewed well will ease an attack.
3. Young dandelion leaves mixed with vinegar will bring relief.
4. A dried potato or conker carried in the pocket delays the onset of rheumatism.

Chilblains — This was another common affliction.
1. The infected area should be beaten with a spray of holly until it bleeds.
2. The chilblains should be anointed with an ointment made from deadly nightshade juice mixed with lard.

Loss of Appetite — This can be counteracted by incorporating rue in the diet.

Haemorrhoids — The pain from these was alleviated by drinking a tea made from alder leaves. Alternatively, the roots of lesser celandine were used. These were gathered, soaked in wine or the urine taken from an ailing man, and then dried. This supposedly provided relief to a sufferer.

Mumps — On the Gloucestershire/Oxfordshire border, a fomentation of marshmallow leaves in boiling water was applied to the swelling.

Warts — The country cures for these were as numerous as the prickles on a rose.

1. The yellow juice of the greater celandine should be rubbed into the wart.
2. A sliced, raw potato bound onto the wart will remove it.
3. A snail should be pricked as many times as the number of warts the sufferer has. The snail should subsequently be stuck on a thorn in the hedgerow. As it dies, the warts will disappear.
4. A wart charmer will use an ash or an elder twig. In this she will cut a notch for each wart and then with her right hand will throw the stick over her left shoulder while telling her patient to forget all about his affliction. In a short time, the warts will vanish.

The Common Cold — This was probably as prevalent in former times as it is today. It was no excuse for a few days off work and so any relief was welcome.

1. Hot cider spiced with rosemary provided a feeling of well-being.
2. Elder flowers were gathered in the spring and dried by suspending them upside down from the kitchen rafters. When required, the dried flowers were made into a tea to be drunk at bedtime. Possibly as an inducement to take the whole dose, any left-overs had to be drunk cold before breakfast the following morning.

May Day

May is traditionally the month of new growth when vegetation burgeons into its summer richness. It is the start of summer with its longer days, a season much welcomed and celebrated by our pagan ancestors.

The original festivities of May Day were to ensure the continued fertility of the countryside, and included the lighting of bonfires, spending the previous night in merry-making in the woods, and bringing back green branches — all symbolic of this new life.

In the seventeenth century, the Puritans recognized the activities for what they originally were — fertility rites — and consequently put an end to most of them. However, the feastday remained in the hearts of the English folk to be revived about two centuries later in an age of greater freedom.

The new festivities differed from those of the earlier times, and the day mainly belonged to the children. Maypoles were set up, sometimes even becoming a permanent fixture as at Chipping Campden and Bledington, but more often they took the form of a stripped birch sapling dragged in from the woods for the day. This was decked with ribbons and garlands of flowers and, to the children dancing and twining the coloured ribbons into intricate patterns, it meant nothing more than a release from the routine of school or labour in the fields. Little known to them, the pole was a fertility symbol and they were merely aping pagan rites. Even the songs gave no hint as to the origin of their frolics, in fact to our modern ears, they sound artificially sweet, the outpourings of a Victorian school ma'am, well illustrated by a Gloucestershire version of a maypole song.

"Round the Maypole, trit-trit-trot,
See what Maypole we have got.
Fine and gay,
Trip away,
Happy is our new May Day."

Perhaps most important to the children was the crowning of the May Queen and her procession around the village and outlying farms accompanied by a May garland. This was usually a wooden framework forming a bell-like structure entirely covered with flowers. Particularly popular were primroses but almost any flower, wild or cultivated could find a niche on the frame. Surprisingly, lady smocks were excluded although they bloomed in profusion at this time of year.

This type of custom was practised with local variations throughout the length and breadth of the English countryside. However, there have been recorded within our own county two different celebrations, one at Randwick and the other, over the river, on May Hill.

In the former, at daybreak, three cheeses were carried in procession on a litter festooned with flowers, to the village church. Here they were rolled three times round the graveyard before being taken to the village green where they were cut up and distributed between the bystanders.

The celebration on May Hill also began at dawn. Parties of young folk gathered from the surrounding area to fight a mock battle, one group representing winter and the other summer. According to the old celtic calendar, May Day was the first day of summer, and so it was always arranged that the summer side would banish that of winter. Fortunately everyone remained friends and, after the "hostilities", returned together in triumph to Newent singing songs declaring that they had brought summer home with them and, as proof, bearing with them all the branches and wild flowers they could carry.

Leafy Battle Field

On Spring Hill, near Snowshill, there was an area of hillside dotted with clumps of beech trees. These were, according to tradition, planted in the same lay-out as that of the various regiments of troops on the field of Waterloo.

Gloucestershire Plant Superstitions

1. A single spray of apple blossom among ripe fruit portends a death in the family.
2. A berried winter means a hard one.
3. It is unlucky to bring white may blossom indoors except on May Day.
4. Snowdrops brought indoors are death omens.
5. An oak coppice is a sinister place after sunset.
6. On May Day, morning dew gathered from a hawthorn bough beautifies a maid for ever.
7. Houseleek growing on a roof protects the building from fire.
8. When gorse is not in flower, kissing is out of season.
9. If herb robert is picked, it is sure to rain.
10. An ash-wood whip stock provides protection against witchcraft.

The Long Lease

A stranger, journeying across country, came to Dudgrove in the south of the county where he found an attractive piece of land which appeared to be unused. He felt the need to settle down after many years on the road, and being in possession of a reasonable sum of money, sought out the owner offering him a good price for the land.

However, the owner was a greedy man and was convinced that the stranger could pay more. He therefore would not agree to the sale, but neither did he refuse.

The stranger was disappointed but, on staying in the area a little longer, was even more determined to acquire that same plot of land. Consequently he went back to the owner who by this time had thought up a clever way of getting a good income.

"I'll allow you the use of the land," said the greedy man, ". . . for a price to be fixed for a period of one harvest. After that a fresh agreement must be drawn up."

By this means, the owner intended getting a good sum of money each year. The two men argued for a long time over the price that the stranger should pay until his first harvest was gathered in. At last both were satisfied. The owner secretly thought he had done very well as he had wrung from the stranger a much higher sum than he had ever expected. Surprisingly, the stranger also seemed satisfied with the deal and went off with a sparkle in his eyes to plant his first crop.

A few weeks later, the owner watched open-mouthed as his tenant unloaded from a farm wagon, basket upon basket of acorns. He was even more dismayed as the man proceeded to plough up the land and carefully plant them.

They grew slowly, first putting up slender shoots, and then slowly —very slowly — growing into oak saplings. Neither the owner nor his tenant lived to see the oak timber harvested. The problem of the long lease was left for their descendants to sort out several generations later.

A few mature oaks, remnants of that first crop, can still be seen growing in the fields between Kempsford and Lechlade.

Midsummer Flower

Midsummer's Eve was a season of magic when country folk believed strange events happened. They thought witches flew in the night sky, and fairies held their revels, feasting and dancing right through the short summer's night until the first cock crowed.

Our pagan ancestors were sun worshippers, and on this day, a mere three days after the longest day of the year, they celebrated the festival of their god. Bonfires were lit in the hope that they would give new strength to the god whose powers, they felt, might be waning as the days began to grow shorter. They also believed that these flames would drive away evil spirits and bring them wealth in the year to come.

Huge bundles of gorse were gathered and set alight, the flaming bundles being carried through their herds of cattle to protect them from illness. Finally, when all the fires had burnt themselves out, the ashes were gathered and scattered on the fields to ensure a good harvest.

The emblem of their god was a plant whose five-petalled yellow flowers resembled the rays of the sun. Not surprisingly, they called it celestial sun. With the spread of Christianity across these islands, Midsummer's Eve was dedicated to St. John the Baptist, and the flower of the old sun god was renamed St. John's wort. The pre-Christian beliefs concerning the power of this plant did not fade with the new religion and, as in many cases, the old creeds became incorporated in the new. The women still went out at Midsummer to gather bunches of this flower now dedicated to a Christian saint, and hung them over the doorways of their cottages and stables to drive away the evil spirits, a fear of which still lurked in the backs of their minds.

The wonderful plant was supposed to possess all sorts of other magical properties. It was said to move if a wicked person came to pick it. Also, provided it was gathered on Midsummer's Eve, it could foretell a young girl's future. If it flourished when placed in her home, she would be married during the coming year. If it withered, she too would be dead before the next Midsummer celebrations.

Gloucestershire Sayings

He's as thick as Tewkesbury mustard.

He looks as if he lives on Tewkesbury mustard.

It's as long coming as Cotswold barley.

He looks as if he hath sold a beane and
bought a peaze.

Beware the fox in an old fearne bush.

It's not spring until you can plant your foot
on twelve daisies.

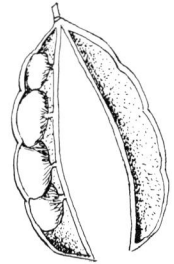

PLANTS AND PURPOSES

A Man's Drink

The fizzy apple drink sold today under the name of cider bears little relationship to that brewed in vast quantities on Gloucestershire farms until relatively recently. The main cider-apple growing area was in the Severn Vale, but even on the thin soils of the sandwiching hills, some fruit was grown. In years when the crop on the Cotswolds was poor, the local farmers would buy vast quantities of apples from the Vale.

Most cider orchards contained a number of different varieties of apple, the trees being left to grow naturally with only infrequent pruning. The harvesting was a crude process, the usual method was by shaking and beating the trees, the fallen fruit being subsequently shovelled up into carts.

The apples were left to sweat in great heaps before being crushed, using a bruising stone rotating in a circular trough. The resulting pulp was pressed and the juice allowed to ferment in casks.

Chunks of raw beef were often placed in the fermenting liquid. This was said to give a better brew. Horrific tales of dead rats improving the flavour were bandied around, although there is little evidence to prove the truth of these stories.

Whatever secret ingredients were included, the resulting brew was carefully tested and pronounced upon by the village worthies. Their approval was important as cider was the chief drink of the farmer and all his men. It was carried to the fields in stone jars or small wooden barrels and lay in the shade of a hedge all day to be drunk when needed. The foremen were given a gallon a day and the labourers half a gallon, this allowance being considered part of their wages.

In the Severn Vale, perry was sometimes provided instead of cider. To many connoisseurs, this was definitely a superior drink — to the layman it was merely a drink made from the fruit of superior trees. Pear trees are taller and more shapely than those of the apple orchards, sometimes reaching a height of fifty or sixty feet. It is said that a single perry-pear tree may bear twenty thousand small fruits. However, a pear orchard takes much longer to mature than a corresponding apple orchard, hence the saying "He who plants pears, plants for his heirs."

Around Chipping Campden, another heady brew was made from the local plums. These were similar to a bullace and produced a drink known as plum jerkum — definitely a man's tipple. The first glass appeared to be pleasant, yet innocuous, tempting the drinker to partake of a second or maybe a third. It was only then that his folly began to show!

Blue Dye from a Yellow Flower

"Matrons and girls among the Britons stain the body
over when taking part in the performance of certain
sacred rites, and rivalling the dusky Ethiopians,
they go naked."

This comment by Pliny the elder is one of the first references to the use of woad by the British. We know little about its cultivation and preparation in those early days, but our information is much more detailed as to its use as a dye, or mordant for other dyes, in the woollen industry of Gloucestershire in later centuries.

The plant is a slender-leaved member of the cabbage family which attains a hcight of two to three feet. Its mass of tiny yellow flowers grow on an upright stem in early summer, and are followed by delicate pods which hang on fine stems to shiver in the lightest of breezes.

The dye was obtained from the leaves which were first picked just before flowering. Further pickings could be made later, but these yielded an inferior product which was treated separately from most of the first harvest.

The leaves were initially spread out to dry in the sun until they could be finely ground to a paste. This was left to ferment, a process which took about a fortnight during a warm summer. The resulting mass was broken up and made into flat cakes which were sprinkled with water and left to ferment further. The final step in the process involved mixing with limewater to enhance the dye properties.

In the early days, the cultivation and processing of the crop was carried out by itinerant workers. Woad cannot easily be grown on the same piece of land for more than two years, and so the travellers would lease a small plot on which they would build temporary shacks to live "on site" as their livelihood flourished around them.

The smell given off by the fermenting plant was highly offensive, impregnating the clothes, hair and even the skin of these workers. It is reported that Queen Elizabeth I was so disgusted by the smell when passing through the county, she ordered that no more of the evil-smelling plant should be sown.

It appears that for once her command was not obeyed and woad continued to be widely cultivated. However, over the ensuing years, cheaper and more permanent dyes were discovered and consequently its presence in the county dwindled until the present day when it is reduced to a few plants growing on the red marl cliffs near Tewkesbury. These flower spasmodically — a sad demise for a plant which contributed so much to the fame of Gloucestershire as an industrial county. Fortunately, its memory is kept alive in the name of Wadfield, a farm on the hills south-east of Winchcombe.

Fire, Fire!

Perhaps the plantain is not one of our most attractive plants and yet once it did a most important job on the farm. When the hay was cut, there would always be plenty of plantain leaves mixed in with the grass and more attractive meadow flowers. After the crop was dried, it was built into a rick from which the farmer deliberately left some of these plantain leaves projecting.

Ricks were always liable to go up in flames if their internal temperature rose too much. The pliability of the plantain leaves varied in a predictable way with rise in temperature, and so periodically, the farmer would pull out some of these leaves and twist them in his hands. If they were completely brittle, his ricks were liable to go up in flames at any moment and should be damped down.

It was this property which gave both the ribwort and greater plantains the local name of "Fireweed".

A Prickly Harvest

It took man many years to invent a mechanical replacement for the teasel in the woollen industry. The spiked seedheads of this strange plant could not be bettered for raising a surface on the felted cloth. Originally the teasel heads were mounted in a frame which the operator dragged down the stretched cloth. Although mechanisation in the industry increased, no substitute was found for the teasels, but it was discovered that the heads could be set on a rotating cylinder.

Dipsacus sativus was the variety of teasel grown for commercial purposes. This differs from the wild variety often seen on roadside verges in that its spines are hooked — the vital factor required to raise the nap of the cloth.

The seed heads were required in vast quantities and, because their cultivation was labour intensive, were usually produced on small family farms. The plant likes a heavy soil and was grown extensively around Tewkesbury, near Cheltenham, and further north where the limestone hills are capped with clay.

The crop was harvested at the end of July and beginning of August, usually by bands of itinerant labourers. The work was hard as the tough stems quickly blunted any knife. The cut teasels could not be stacked as this broke the valuable spines, and so they were fastened on poles to dry.

The first record of teasel growing in Gloucestershire was in 1812 when they were marketed at twopence per thousand heads. It seems that cultivation ceased in the early days of the Second World War, probably because the land was required for food production.

A Pickling Harvest

Samphire grew extensively on the New Grounds. It was collected for either pickling or making into a medicine.

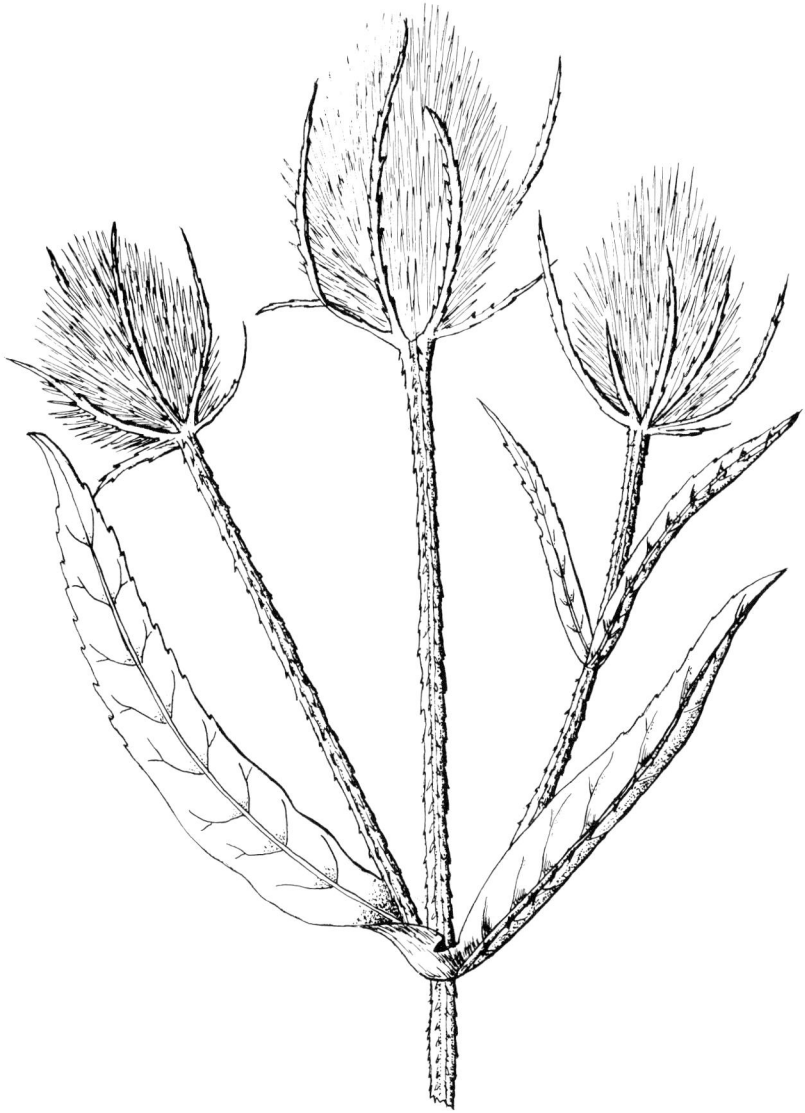

Vernacular Names

How much more picturesque are the countryman's names for a flower than the formal English ones and the even less attractive double-barrelled latin nomenclature. These obviously have a place in formal botany textbooks, but sadly have ousted many delightful dialect names for the plants of the countryside.

Most people have some affection for wild flowers (whether or not they can give a name to them is a different matter), and there is no shame in this. A child making a daisy chain, an old man commenting that the apple blossom is not what it used to be, a dog walker noting that a familiar clump of cow parsley is in flower earlier than normal, and a hiker perhaps complaining about the overpowering smell of wild garlic — all these are observing the world of flowers in their own way, a way suited to twentieth-century living.

How much more aware of the world of flowers was the housewife of former centuries who of necessity knew her wild flowers — which could be eaten, which were poisonous and which cured what ailments. They were part of her everyday life. Similarly, the farm labourer knew which plants blunted his scythe, which ones would poison his cattle and which would dry to make a nutritious hay.

For one's own use, it is not necessary to be able to give a name to any particular flower, but when talking to another person, there must be some given name to distinguish it from others. For example, a seventeenth century housewife, having found a new patch of self heal, which was used to prevent wounds from turning septic, would refer to it to her neighbour as carpenter's herb, as woodworkers, being particularly prone to gashes, always had a bunch of it in their workshop.

Several plants were similarly given names relating to their medicinal use. The greater celandine was known as wartwort as its juice was applied to warts, and the insidious ground elder was called goutweed, being used to cure that ailment.

Other plants were given names describing their appearance. The powers of observation and imagination of the country folk of the past were surely far superior to those of today, for they gave names such as granny's nightcap (columbine), candlemas bells (snowdrop), town hall clock (moschatel — wonderfully descriptive of the four outwardly-facing flowers) and weasel's snout (yellow archangel).

Names indicative of the time of year the plants bloomed were also common. Many spring flowers included the word cuckoo in their vernacular name, showing they were present at the time the cuckoo began to sing again. In Gloucestershire, wood sorrel boasted three such names — cuckoo's victuals, cuckoo's bread and cheese, and cuckoo's meat. Greater stitchwort was called wedding flowers as most weddings took place in the spring when it was in flower, and, at the other end of the season, common ragwort was known as summer farewell.

There is poetry in many of the old names which make them easy on the tongue and pleasant to the ear. How sad that old local names such as paradise plant (mezereon), Billy button (red campion), mother-of-thousands (ivy-leaved toadflax), and popple (poppy), have vanished from our children's vocabularies.

Deadly Beauty

"If the traveller has a fine afternoon at his disposal, he should not fail to ride up the valley from Daneway Bridge to Tunley. The steep bank on the right is bright with masses of yellow ragwort and golden rod, and among them are growing great bushes of deadly nightshade (Atropa belladonna). The livid purple flowers are now over, but the black cherry-like fruit is lurking in abundance beneath the broad handsome leaves. So tempting is its appearance that the plant has often been destroyed by the country people in places where their truant children might chance to fall a prey to it.

H. A. Evans — 1905
(Highways and Byways in Oxford and the Cotswolds)

Strange Uses for Everyday Plants

Lady's Bedstraw — This was mixed with nettle juice to act as rennet and give colouring to Double Gloucester cheese.

Mullein — The soft leaves of this plant were used to pad hard, unyielding boots.

Wych Elm — The wood of this tree was used to make arrows, while long strips of its bark were used to secure thatch.

Ash — Its wood was used to make otter spears.

Horse Tail — The stems of this strange plant have a high silica content which makes them very abrasive. It was therefore used as a pan scourer and for smoothing off woodwork and plaster mouldings.

Dogwood — The local name for this hedgerow shrub was skiver tree derived from its use for making skewers.

Reeds — These were packed between the staves of cider barrels to make them water-tight.

Juniper — The perfume of the berries of this shrub was supposed to purify the air and guard cottages from the "Evil Eye".

Holly — Witnesses in the Mine Law Court in the Forest of Dean took the oath while touching the Bible with a sprig of holly. This is said to have originated so that they did not soil the Bible with their grimy hands. The same twig was always used — being considered as consecrated to this purpose by long usage.

Unusual Decorations

Christmas — We always think of the mistletoe as the plant beneath which kisses are exchanged but, in Gloucestershire, the holly served a similar function during the early part of the nineteenth century. A bough of the evergreen was brought into the kitchen of a big house where it was suspended from the ceiling near the centre of the room. According to a local writer of the time, this rendered every female passing beneath it, subject to the salutation of any men in the room. What form this salutation took is not revealed. Occasionally the bush would be decorated with mistletoe and ivy dipped in blue bag and white starch — perhaps it then gave a double reason for "saluting" a passing lady!

Early Spring — A spray of hawthorn before it came into leaf was set upright in a pot of moss. For this decoration it was important that it carried plenty of undamaged thorns. Flowerheads of white and purple violets were stuck alternately on the spines until the bare twig was apparently converted into a spring-flowering bush.

Christmas Again — During the winter, the seed heads of wild oats can be found in hedgerows. These hang over and bear long, hairy spines which once formed the basis of a strange decoration. The seeds were stuck into a turnip to entirely cover its surface and were arranged with the spines sticking out to give it the appearance of a hedgehog. The odd creature was stuck onto the top of an unlit candle and placed on the mantlepiece to form the centrepiece of the Christmas decorations in the servants' hall of a big house.

Hedge Laying

From the edge of the Cotswold scarp, look out over the Severn Vale. Below will be a patchwork pattern of fields, their seams marked by miles of hedgerow. These are a man-made feature of our landscape and have developed to their present form after centuries of care by successive landowners.

The benefits of a well-managed hedge were twofold. Firstly, they were stockproof and prevented livestock from straying. Secondly, they gave the animals shelter from wind and sun.

Traditional management of a hedge involved periodic laying (or layering) which prevented it from becoming thin at the bottom. However, this is a labour intensive process which occupied many farm hands throughout the winter months when other work on the land was scarce. Nowadays, mechanised cutting is much faster, but results in a hedge which is very sparse in its lower parts — a defect which is corrected by the extensive use of barbed wire or electric fences.

The art of hedge laying — and indeed it is an art — involves removing all of the undergrowth and cutting out much of the old wood. The hedger then trims the sides of the hedge before beginning the really skilled stage. In this, he cuts almost through the remaining main stems close to the ground, but leaving sufficient bark intact for the sap to rise in the spring. The stems are bent over so that they lie almost parallel to the ground. He drives in stakes, selected and cut from the discarded wood, at intervals of approximately two feet, and between these weaves the bent over stems. Finally, the job is completed by using long, flexible pieces of willow, wych elm, or hazel, to bind the top in a neat basketwork pattern. This is sometimes called "feathering".

The pattern of the final hedge varies according to its proposed use. A hedge for containing cattle must be stronger and taller than one for sheep. The latter however, must be interwoven right down to ground-level as a sheep can squeeze through any tiny gap, hence the saying, "What sheep can see through, they'll go through".

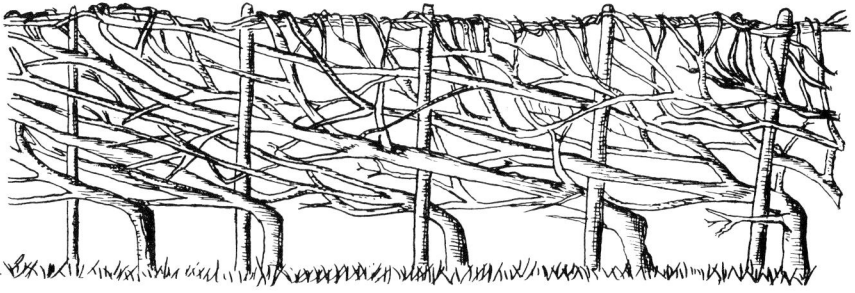

Midlands Hedge (to retain cattle)

Welsh Hedge (to retain sheep)

More Uses

Blackthorn wood was traditionally used for making walking sticks.

Elder pith was used to clean pewter.

Bluebell sap was used to stick the flight feathers on arrows.

Gloucestershire Wine Recipes

Dandelion Wine

Ingredients: 4 quarts dandelion heads
4 quarts boiling water
3 lbs loaf sugar
1 inch whole ginger
1 lemon
1 tablespoon brewer's yeast moistened with water
1 orange (rind only)

Method: Pour the boiling water over the petals of the flowers. Leave the bowl covered for several days remembering to stir well frequently. Strain the liquid from the petals and pour it into a preserving pan. Add the lemon juice and the rind of both the lemon and orange cut into thin strips. Then add the ginger and sugar. Boil gently for an hour and allow to cool. When at about body temp. add the yeast on a slice of toast. Allow to stand for two weeks when all effervescence should have stopped. Siphon off the liquid and transfer to a cask which should be well bunged down for a year. After this time, bottle, and, if possible, keep for one to two years before drinking.

Sloe and Blackberry Wine

Ingredients: 3 lbs sloes
2 lbs blackberries
1 gallon water
3 lb sugar per gallon liquid

Method: Boil the water and pour it over the fruit. Let the mixture stand for a fortnight and then add the sugar. When dissolved strain through muslin into a cask and allow it to work fully before bottling.

Castlett Sloe Wine

Ingredients: 3 pints sloes
1 gallon water
3 lb sugar (preferably lump)

Method: Place the sloes in an earthenware pan and pour the boiling water over them. Allow to stand for at least ten days, stirring frequently. Strain through a fine muslin. Add the sugar and put into a cask. Allow to work before bunging up, retaining some to fill up the cask as it bubbles over.

Lower Slaughter Cowslip Wine

Ingredients: 1 quart of cowslip flowers
1 gallon water
4 lb sugar
1/2 pennyworth of yeast
1 lemon

Method: Put the flowers into a bag in a stewpan and boil in the water for one and a half hours. Press and add the sugar to the liquid, reheating until the sugar dissolves. Allow to cool to blood heat and then add the lemon juice and yeast. The wine can be bottled the following morning.
(This sounds a highly explosive mixture!)

This wine is supposed to induce a new-born foal to suck. However, it is not recommended for conservation reasons on account of the large numbers of cowslip flowers required.

Woodwaxen

A plant which can be found in clayland pastures is the dyers' greenweed. Seldom is it eaten by cattle and in late summer its elegant yellow flowers provide wonderful splashes of colour in a countryside perhaps browning after a period of drought. Not always though has it been allowed to bloom undisturbed for once it was the subject of the "Woodwaxen" harvest.

Poor folk would go out and collect the plant by cartloads in July. Women particularly undertook the work which was very hard as the plant had to be pulled up by the roots which were strongly embedded in the heavy soil. The pay was not great, but was enhanced by the practice of watering the load. The woodwaxers would claim this was to keep their harvest green, but the local dyers who bought the loads claimed it was to increase its weight.

Eventually, the plant was overharvested, there being no records of it ever being planted as a crop. Farmers also discouraged the picking of it on their lands as, although in itself not palatable, it provided shelter for the growth of young grass during the lean months of early spring.

The main use of the weed was in the preparation of woollen cloths to receive other dyes. It yields a dull yellow colour to the raw cloth which can subsequently be dipped into other liquors to produce a whole range of greens.

Fuel for Free

Fields known as Poor's Lot were places where village folk could go to cut furze for heating their bread ovens. They were small patches of land left over from the time when common lands were enclosed.

Osier Beds

At one time, basket making was an important industry in the Severn Vale. The raw materials for this craft were willow wands obtained from osier beds. Today, with the increased use of plastics, there is little call for the woven baskets, fish traps, farm hurdles and garden furniture formerly made by village craftsmen.

Little evidence remains of the once extensive osier beds, except at a few scattered locations where they are sadly neglected and overgrown, suitable only for nesting birds. Nowadays, the nearest working beds are on the Somerset Levels where remnants of the industry still survive.

When active, the osier beds were planted using cuttings from mature trees. These were stuck into deep-ploughed, well-manured ground just sufficiently far apart that the intervening ground could be weeded. The young trees were pruned at the end of their first season of growth, the shoots being long enough for harvesting by the end of their third year. A bed could be worked for many years, producing "stools" which increased in size each year, and from which the young shoots could be harvested every three years.

The shoots were cut in winter after the sap had gone down, the harvested rods being stacked and then bundled. They could be used in various ways. Green rods were not treated before use, and were used for making hurdles. Brown rods become coloured when either air dried or steamed. These were used for rustic garden chairs and coarse baskets. White rods were definitely at the superior end of the market. These were stored in pits from harvest time right through until May and were subsequently stripped to remove the bark.

In Gloucestershire, basket-making was especially important in the fruit growing areas where hampers were made to carry the fruit safely to distant markets. Apples, pears and plums were packed in large hampers known as pots. Because of different packing densities, a "pot" held differing weights of fruit. Typically, a plum pot held 90lbs, an apple pot 84lbs, and a pear pot 100lbs.

Another local use was for making putchers, which were long, open-weave, tapering baskets used by the Severn fishermen for trapping both eels and salmon.

What the Doctor Ordered!

Even until the end of the nineteenth century, most villages still had their quack who claimed to be able to cure man and animal alike by the use of herbs. The following is the advice given by the "doctor" from Ablington:-

"First of all you must know that the elder is good for anything in the world, but especially for swellings. If you put some of the leaves on your face, they will cure toothache in five minutes. Then for the nerves there's nothing like the berries of ivy. Yarrow makes a splendid ointment; and be sure and remember Soloman's seal for bruises, and comfrey for "hurts" and broken bones. Camomile cures indigestion, and ash-tree buds make a stout man thin. Soak some ash leaves in hot water, and you will have a drink that is better than any tea, and destroys "gravel". Walnut-tree bark is a splendid emetic; and mountain flax, which grows everywhere in the Cotswolds, is uncommon good for the 'innards'. 'Ettles (nettles) is good for stings. Damp them and rub them onto a "wapse" sting and they will take away the pain directly."

A Cotswold Village
J. Arthur Gibbs (1898)

A Bit of Gretton Doggerel

Daffy-down-dilly
What grows by the well.
A very purty flower,
With a nasty smell.

112

PLANTS AND POSTERITY

Where to Next?

In the closing years of the 1980s, it is fashionable to be "green", to consider our environment and offer political solutions to prevent destruction of life as we know it.

Unfortunately, it is largely our present way of living with expectations of all modern conveniences which has brought about the necessity for this. In the past, man did not consciously protect his surroundings, rather he lived in harmony with them, giving back to the land as much as he took from it. However, the concept of conservation is not totally new, only its popularity. In 1829, J. L. Knapp, a local diarist, wrote:-

> "Even in our own days, heaths, moors and wilds have disappeared so as to leave no indications of their former state but the name."

It was during the nineteenth century that both the study of botany and the practice of botanical drawing became popular among the educated classes. Books recording the flora of particular areas were published, Gloucestershire not being neglected in this field. In 1844, a Flora for the Cheltenham area was produced, entitled "Botanical Guide to the Environs of Cheltenham". This lists several flowers which have now vanished completely from the region, and also records several more as "common" which now occur only sparingly in the vicinity.

In 1871, another Flora was published for the Forthampton district. This was compiled by W. P. Serocold and rejoices in the title of "List of the Flowering Plants of the Parish of Forthampton and its Neighbourhood." Three hundred species are listed with comments by each concerning its frequency, location, or any particular characteristics of the plant. Orpine (a member of the sedum family) is said to occur on the bank by Forthampton Church where it seldom comes to flower, because the heads are cut off by boys before it blooms.

Home wine making is at present enjoying renewed popularity, and substitutes have been found for the cowslip. However, as fields of dandelions, at present considered a weed, are ravaged for feeding repacious demi-johns, some thought must be given to these beautiful blooms. Is it possible they could go the same way as the cowslip? It seems impossible, and yet these are exactly the same thoughts as our forebears had about the cowslip.

Tree felling is also a contentious matter. Most woods are managed to produce a crop of timber, in which case the trees must be felled while at the peak of their condition, and not when subject to decay. Despite this knowledge, it is still a sad sight to see a forest giant crashing to the ground or lying with an identification tag stapled to its tell-tale rings.

F. Duckworth, in 1908, recalled how, in an earlier century, royal intervention had saved some of Gloucestershire's woodlands.

> "Twice royalty has visited the neighbourhood (Painswick). In 1535 Anne Boleyn and Henry VIII came hither on a hunting expedition from Gloucester, and Henry was much shocked when he heard that the Lord of the Manor, Lord Lisle, had contracted to fell four hundred of his trees. It is possible Henry VIII appreciated the beauty of the landscape; it is certain he was afraid of having his sport spoilt. He promptly ordered Lord Lisle to cut his contract rather than his woods. If only Henry could be restored to life in this our day, just long enough to put a stop to the felling of Buckholt Woods!"

Advancing into the twentieth century, Gloucestershire became the adopted home of a keen conservationist — Algernon Gissing —whose ideas were well in advance of others of his time. In his book "The Footpath Way in Gloucestershire", he commented:

> "A pressed and labelled specimen, except for study in some established collection, is a wretched substitute for the precious living plant which we can have a delightful ramble to look at. If we take only the flower without the root we have in all likelihood prevented its seeding, and so multiplying itself several-fold the following year . . .There are after all hundreds of lovely flowers that we call common, of which we may bring home a handful for pleasure or study without any uneasy feeling that we are robbing a beautiful landscape of any of its interest or charm, and in all probability with the positive merit of discovering some fresh beauty that we had so long ignored before."

Certainly, his first premise is still sound advice, but the second, about picking a handful of common flowers is more debatable as it poses the question "What is common?" An old countrywoman recently interviewed said that in her youth, she had thought nothing of picking several buckets full of cowslip heads for making wine. These flowers were considered common and people found it impossible to imagine the spring countryside without fields full of them.

It was not only this heavy picking, but also changes in agricultural practice which led to a drastic decline in the numbers of cowslips, a trend which was only arrested by giving them legal protection. Fortunately, in Gloucestershire at least, this story seems to have a happy ending, for in recent years numbers have begun to increase again.

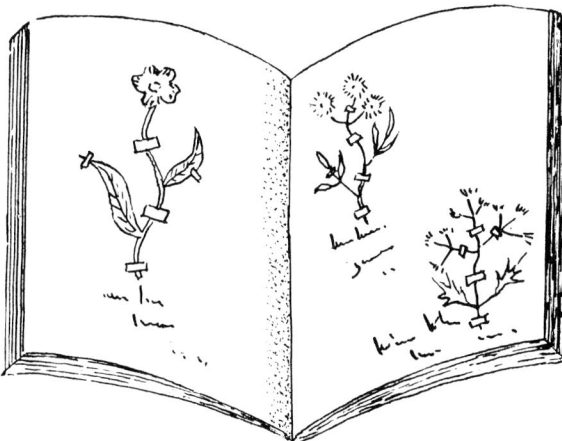

About thirty years later, in her book "Country Contentments", Margaret Westerling wrote on the same theme:

"So much of the old woodland is now being felled, sometimes without apparent reason. There was a wood near Birdlip long known to me as a sanctuary of rare and lovely flowers, a spot I visited yearly because of them — lily of the valley, Soloman's seal, helleborine, the tall spikes of habenaria — all grew there, with spindlewood and hazel over them, and beeches for taller shade. When I passed a few days ago, I saw with a shock that every tree had gone, and with them all the beauty of that corner, full of so much that we are slowly but surely destroying. Plants sometimes die for lack of the shade and secrecy the trees had given."

Again, modern forms of transport have much to answer for in the rape of the countryside. Most roads have now been tarred, their dark surfaces causing many old countrymen to bemoan the passing of the old white roads. Eva Dobell, a local poet, wrote in her poem "Cotswold Roads":-

"Those broad hill roads that lead away
Dusty and white, with margins wide
Of grass and myriad upland flowers —
Jewelled bands on either side."

But it is not only the change in road surface which has altered the face of the countryside, it is the vehicles which travel along them. Lorries of a size never envisaged when the roads were made, hurtle along them, making road-widening frequently necessary, the land for this usually being stolen from the flower-rich verges. Additionally, the plants growing at the side of the roads are often smothered in dust and other pollution from the passing traffic. An old song summed it up in the following words:-

"The rich go by in their madcap machinery,
They kicks up the dust and they spoils all the greenery."

117

However, it must always be remembered that the present plant population has evolved in a man-made landscape. It has been modified according to man's changing needs, and it must never be imagined that we can stop the clock at any time to prevent further change. Some plants will die out in the county, others will come in, possibly foreign invaders brought in with bird seed, agricultural products or even on the wheels of cars taken abroad on a family holiday.

Specific species can be saved by protection of their habitat, as we have seen with the Badgeworth buttercup (see page 53). This is possible where the area concerned is small, and even then only with careful treatment. Conservation is a much misunderstood word. Many people consider that a nature reserve is a piece of land merely left to "go wild". However, this process would in time completely change the nature of the land. In fact, the reserve must be carefully managed, if possible in the same way as it has been for centuries.

An example of this has recently been observed on Walmore Common, on the flood plain to the west of the River Severn. Part of the common was traditionally harvested to provide thatching reeds, but with the decrease in the demand for thatch, the reeds were left unharvested. This, together with the drop in the water-table, brought about by improved drainage, has resulted in a reduction in the marsh-loving flowers which once thrived there.

Many areas of special botanical interest are in the caring hands of the Gloucestershire Trust for Nature Conservation, one of the many local Trusts which cover the entire country. They are responsible for the management of Nature Reserves, while another organisation — The Gloucestershire Naturalists' Society — keeps records of plants growing anywhere in the county. This enables the health of any plant species to be ascertained and hopefully indicates early signs of any declining populations so that measures can be taken to stop the downward trend in numbers if it is thought necessary.

In spite of all the present-day pressures, Gloucestershire is still a county rich in flowers and trees. It is up to us to ensure that those who come after us inherit this birthright so that they too, can enjoy Gloucestershire's Green Heritage.

The Country Code

Guard against all risk of fire
Fasten all gates
Keep dogs under proper control
Keep to paths across farmland
Avoid damaging fences, hedges and walls
Leave no litter
Safeguard water supplies
Protect wildlife, wild plants and trees
Go carefully along country roads
Respect the life of the countryside

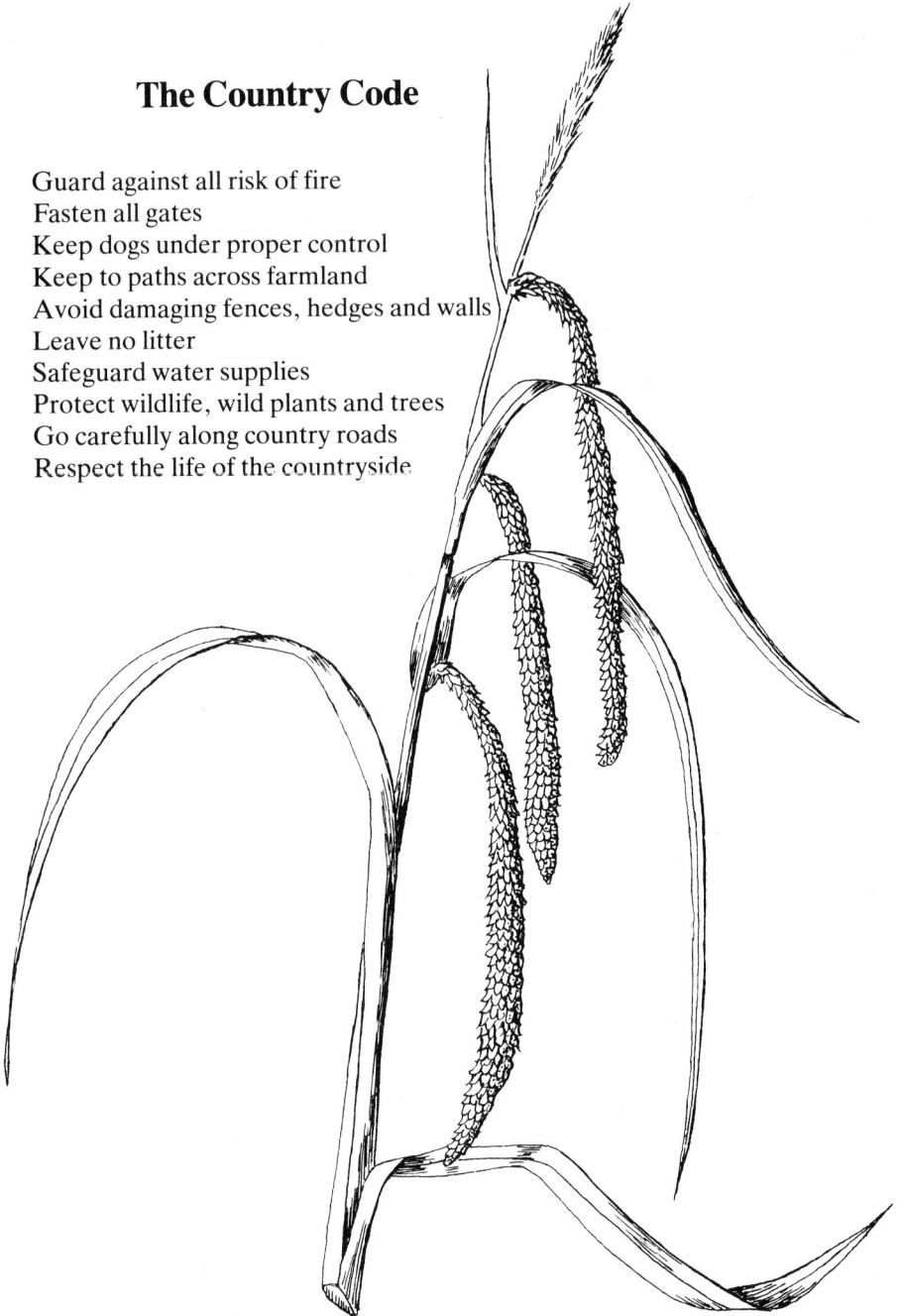